Community Library of DeWitt & Jamesville
5110 Jamesville Road
DeWitt, NY 13078

Find Your Roots Now!

A Step by Step Guide for Beginning Genealogists

Joe Long

No part of this publication may be reproduced, distributed, or transmitted without the prior written permission of the publisher except for brief quotations embodied in critical reviews.
©2017 Joe Long
Published by First Run Press

Find Your Roots Now!
ISBN: 978-0-9766816-9-4
firstrunpress@yahoo.com

Contents

Genealogy As A Hobby	1
Setting Goals	4
It's All About You	7
The Land of the Living	10
Organization, Organization, Organization	13
The Local Library	19
Documenting Your Sources	22
County Governmental Records	25
National Archives Records – Census	31
National Archives Records – Immigration	37
National Archives Records – Military	41
Federal and State Land Records	47
Church Records	54
Genealogical Software	57
Free On-Line Databases	60
A Picnic at the Cemetery	63
Genealogical Societies	68
Immigrant Ancestors	75
Hiring Professional Genealogists	85
Genealogy and DNA	89
Publishing Your Work	93
Glossary	98
Index	101

Introduction

Mankind has always had a special interest in the past, especially family history. If you always wondered about your past, where certain family traits originated, or whether those stories about a royal line or a family ancestor are true, you are not alone. Millions have begun searching their roots to answer these questions and more. Internet technology and DNA testing have provided new tools to help locate those long-lost ancestors and to document information uncovered.

Additionally, we can now reach out to other researchers anywhere on the globe for input and information. Suppose your family originally came from Germany in the late 1800s. Wouldn't it be great to trace your family back to their original home in Germany and then find living descendants of your tree still living in the same town? They may have original bible records or other documents taking the family back many more generations. Plus, what a great vacation trip to visit the homeland and meet your new cousins! Many family researchers have done just that, plus much more. This guide will get you started in the right direction with proven techniques developed over many years. Here are some of the tools you will learn:

- How to get started organizing your search
- Recordkeeping and documentation
- Using the Web wisely
- Avoiding the Internet trap
- Getting past research roadblocks
- Using census and military records
- Proper source citation
- Using government records
- DNA and genealogy
- Publishing your family history project

Now Let's get started!

Find Your Roots Now!

Chapter 1
Genealogy as a Hobby

Any family tree produces some lemons, some nuts and a few bad apples.
--Anonymous

Where do I fit into the big picture? How did my ancestors contribute to who I am today? What were they like? How did they view the world? Mankind has always been curious about the past.

Most of us grew up at least knowing our grandparents. A few are lucky to have known great-grandparents. Beyond that, unless you are very curious, you might not have asked anyone in your family about ancestors. Some lucky families have a famous ancestor, or are related to royalty. However, most of us spring from a line of "commoners" who worked, lived and died in virtual obscurity. The thing that makes them important is that they are your ancestors and you would not be here today if it were not for their decision to have children. And those children had children and on down the line to you. We owe it to our ancestors to know more about them. As we learn about them, we learn about ourselves.

A Brief History

Genealogy as a pastime has changed dramatically over the years. Past genealogists were primarily concerned with proving a connection to aristocracy and royalty. Family pedigrees were only maintained for the upper classes of Europe until census and other records became more common for all classes in the early 16th century.

In the United States, early work was done by John Farmer with his book, *A Genealogical Register of the First Settlers of New England*, published in 1829. In 1845, the first genealogical society was formed, called The New England Historic Genealogical Society. The National Genealogical Society was formed in 1903 with 24 charter members. The Society today has thousands of members.

Donald Lines Jacobus helped develop sound scientific methods to compile family history by using original records and a critical approach to research. With the advent of computers and the Internet, much more information is available to individuals at their fingertips. However, primary research is still the correct way to find the right information on your ancestor. You must question all data before adding it to your file. (See Sources in Chapter 7).

Today, genealogy is one of the most popular hobbies in the U.S.A. As a society, we are asking more questions about where we came from and who we are. It is estimated that over 80 million Americans are actively involved in family research. If you are just starting your work in family history, the fun is just beginning. However, be forewarned, once you get the "bug" you are hooked for life!

Learn About Your Past and Yourself

Once you begin the journey, you will look at the world in a whole new way. You will realize that mankind has created a complex system of laws, government and regulations over the years with which your ancestors had to deal. However, if it were not for the law, we may not have any trace of their existence. I'm sure you will agree, in today's world, almost every step we take is documented and recorded in some way. Our descendants will have no trouble finding information about us. The difficulty for you is identifying the appropriate records to fill in the missing pieces in your family tree puzzle.

In the past, it was much more common for only a few events in a person's life to be recorded...birth, marriage and death. The further back in time you go, the less documentation exists and you must use other sources to find your ancestors. Luckily, early in our history as a nation, historians realized the importance of preserving records that might be needed for future generations. Key government officials dealing with land, military records and tax records generally tried to find ways to protect records from harm.

There were a few disasters, such as floods, fire, war and other events that caused some records to be partially or fully destroyed. I have spent many a day working in Southern courthouses that were burned during the Civil War. Almost the entire 1890 U.S. census was destroyed by fire. As recently as 1973, a disastrous fire destroyed approximately 16-18 million Official Military Personnel Files at the National Personnel Records Center in St. Louis.

You will find your past is made up of a great cast of characters. Just as in modern families, there were "good" and "not-so-good" members. Your great-great aunt Martha may have gotten married several times or great-great grandfather Bob may have been the town drunk. However, that just makes the digging more interesting. So what if they weren't perfect people? They had problems and challenges just like we do today. In your research, you may find a family secret that has been covered up for many many years. You must ask yourself if you are willing to reveal the truth to other family members or "let sleeping dogs lie". A few skeletons in the closet can make your research that much more interesting and bring a new perspective to your ancestors and to your own place in the world.

Enjoy the Journey!

As you get started, remember that this is a fun, rewarding hobby that will bring years of enjoyment to your life. And keep in mind...you can never be completely finished. There will always be more bones to dig up! You will spend countless hours working on one family line that seems to have hit a brick wall. Then, when you are about to give up, you find a new clue, a new book or you remember something your grandmother told you, and voilà! you find the breakthrough you needed. I have spent years working to find the parents of some distant ancestor, only to discover the answer was easily accessible, but I hadn't yet opened the right door!

Your present is made up of little parts of your ancestors' past. Your research will bring your own family closer together. Family vacations can include a visit to the places your ancestors lived, battlefields where they once fought, and cemeteries where they now sleep in eternal slumber. You might even find that your children will better appreciate history when it becomes more personal and fun.

You will discover the euphoria of finding that long lost relative and their entire family on a microfilm census record, or the name of the ship that brought your immigrant ancestor to America.

Your research will become part of history. You may find that you are the first person in your family to construct a family tree. Your legacy will be appreciated for generations to come. Future researchers will build on your work and help complete a few more branches. At some point, DNA testing (See Chapter 20) may determine our ancestral lines back to Adam and Eve. But for now, it's done one generation at a time!

Chapter 2
Setting Goals

I want to find ALL of them! So far I only have a few thousand.
--Anonymous

How do you know when you've reached your destination?

Before jumping in with both feet, it might be a good time to think about your goals. Do you want to trace your family back to the immigrant ancestor?...to four generations? Are you working on a membership to a lineage society or just having fun in your spare time? Since there are so many routes you can take, it is good to define your goals so you can monitor your progress.

Some researchers concentrate only on their surname, taking that line back as far as possible. Others take each family line back as far as possible concentrating on the direct lines (parents, grandparents, etc.), not indirect lines (children of children, of aunts and uncles and cousins). Five generations represent 31 individuals (including yourself) going back over 150 years. The fifth generation would be your great-great grandparents. Finding all 31 individuals is an ambitious goal that may take you a few months to complete, or many years of hard work!

You may want to begin a family newsletter that covers various historical items of interest. Some newsletters have grown to cover thousands of descendants with a common surname or ancestor. You might just want to include a few close relatives with the hope of generating interest in future research, announcing a family reunion or preserving oral history from older relatives.

Time and Energy
We all have less spare time in this busy world. To keep focused on your research, you must determine how much time you are willing to commit. When you can spend the time to make trips to the library and to your distant relatives and to add to your research notes. Luckily with the advent of computers and the Internet, you can practically continue your research twenty-four hours a day! However, your family might get a little concerned with your sanity. Set reasonable goals that allow you to enjoy your hobby while taking care of everyday commitments. It is always a good idea to step back from your research and think about what you need to make the next big breakthrough. Just discussing your roadblocks with others can help find the solution. The key to success is a balanced approach.

Writing a Book

If your ultimate goal is to write a book, there are several things to consider:

- Target audience
- Single or multi-family focus
- Number of generations included
- Collaboration from others
- Photos and other memorabilia
- Personal interviews

Like your genealogical research, your book must stop somewhere. It may be easier to set those limits now before time goes by and you are no closer to a finished book than when you began. (For more information, see Chapter 21).

Learning about History

One of the extra benefits of researching your family is the historical knowledge you will gain. You will find that your ancestors lived in historic times and were part of the events that shaped America. One of the most fascinating aspects of my research was the tracing of migrating families across the US. My ancestors must have either been very restless or local trouble makers, because they never stayed put for more than one generation. They felt the pull of new lands and new opportunities that took them westward.

Unless your family members were recent immigrants to America, or stayed in one place, you will experience the same result. As new lands were opened for settlement, pioneers moved across America looking for the perfect spot to start a farm or a new business. As the Civil war erupted, families took sides primarily along the Mason-Dixon Line. Thus, families who may have lived and intermarried on the eastern seaboard of the US now are on opposite sides of the conflict just a few decades later. You may even find family names that fought against each other in a Civil War battle, and then would later intermarry as they trekked westward. Your research will bring life to your ancestors when you realize the struggle they endured to create a better life for their family.

Chapter Action Plan

- Define your goals
- Determine how much time you can devote to research
- Schedule your research time weekly and stick with it
- If possible, schedule business and family trips to locations that will aid your research
- Begin asking relatives if anyone else has already completed some family research

Chapter 3
It's All About You!

If man cares not for his roots, then how can he care for his branches?
--Doyle M. Davis

Now that you have prepared yourself for the journey ahead, it's time to get organized, and begin the process. Surprisingly, it begins with you. Remember, this history will include you, and in the future, some genealogist will be trying to learn about you. Make it easy for them by keeping a record to pass down to future generations.

Write Your Autobiography
Many individuals keep journals or diaries of their thoughts, activities and milestones. This is an excellent way to add substance to your life story. If a journal is not your style, at least sit down and write out a timeline of your life so far. Include when and where you were born, your parents and grandparents names and things you can remember about your early childhood, including where you lived, your friends' names, your pets' names and anything you experienced that would help a future researcher understand the real you!

Include your education history, such as where you went to school, your favorite teachers, subjects and any special activities such as sports, band or drama you enjoyed. Who was your date to the prom? Who was your best friend in school? Where do you attend college? Military experience, first job, first house, first marriage...you get the picture.

You should also make an audio or video of your fondest memories. Have someone interview you about your life. Start at the beginning and move forward through time. Discuss how your name was selected. Are you named after relatives, family friends, or a famous person? If you parents are still alive, they might want to add their input on this. Do you have a nickname? Discuss the house you grew up in and your favorite memories. This will be treasured items for future generations. (See Chapter 4 for tips on recording an interview).

Gather Photos and Mementos
Go through your old photos and pick out your favorites of your parents, grandparents, siblings and your childhood friends. Include your birthdays, special events, sports and other photos you feel will help tell your story. What if something tragic happened to you tomorrow? What would you want people to know about your life and your history? Perhaps you were an Eagle Scout or captain of the cheerleading squad. You may have served in the military or received a scholarship to study in Europe.

Any keepsakes or mementos will help complete your story. Be sure and discuss these items on your audio or video diary so others will understand their significance. Don't wait until "someday" because it may be too late. I'm sure you wish your great-grandparents had sat down with someone to tell their life story before it was too late for them. Create an album of your photos. If you have access to a computer and scanner, you might want to scan them into a file for future preservation and inclusion in your family history file.

Documentation

You will learn the habits that will serve you well as you complete your family tree. You must document everything! Let me repeat, document everything! Pretend you are going before a judge and must prove your case in court. What evidence will you present to convince the jury your research is sound? That is what you must do with your own life story. Include copies of birth and marriage records, baptismal, confirmation, diplomas. You want to build your file with as many official documents as possible. Dig through those drawers, closets and file cabinets to get what you need to prove you are who you claim you are before the court. As with your photos, you will want to make copies or scan them to create a permanent file. Create a file folder with your name on the tab. This is where you will add your personal notes, copies of documents, certificates and copies of your photos. You will create a similar file folder for each family in your tree. If you don't have a file cabinet, you might want to purchase one. If you are concerned about fire or other hazards, you might want to invest in a fire safe or plan on keeping your original documents in a safe deposit box. You will also need the following items:

- 3" Three-ring binder
- Several 8 ½" X 11" notepads
- Dividers for your binder
- Audio and/or video recording equipment and digital storage media

Leave Your Legacy

Your research will become the research of future generations. Provide them a well-documented, thorough report that will stand the test of time. Don't cut corners or reach unsubstantiated conclusions. Remember to always take personal recollections with a grain of salt, to be verified with additional documentation. Never trust a computer-generated family tree from a distant relative unless it comes with proper documentation, or you can prove the results independently. A false genealogy is worse than no genealogy at all! Don't forget that once your family history is in print, it will be taken as gospel by future readers. Use the methods outlined in this book and by other professionals in the field. Learn from the mistakes of others and get started on the right foot even if you must work a little harder to prove that elusive fact.

Chapter Action Plan

- Write your own autobiography
- Make copies of your birth certificate, marriage license and other government issued documents
- Create an album of photos detailing your life history
- Create your genealogy binder for research materials
- Create a file folder for each family
- Document everything and don't cut corners on research

Chapter 4
The Land of the Living

My family consists of in-laws and outlaws
--Anonymous

Talk with your Relatives
Where do you start? The best place is with your older living relatives. After you have completed your personal history, you can now do the same for others. Start with your parents and move on to your grandparents. If they are deceased, contact other relatives, such as aunts, uncles, great-aunts and great-uncles.

Talk to anyone who may know about past generations in your family. Be tactful in your approach. Older family members may be sensitive about discussing the past if it brings up painful memories. If possible, visit them in person. They may be much more relaxed than talking by phone. If you can't travel to them, write a brief, succinct letter that outlines exactly what you want to know.

Here is an outline of what you want to discover:

- When and where they were born
- Their parents and grandparents' full names
- Where they grew up and where they lived
- When they were married and to whom
- The names of their children
- Where and when their children were born
- Interesting events in their lives
- If anyone in the family has already compiled a family history or has access to family bibles, old photographs, family heirlooms or other important items

Recording the Interview
If possible, sit down and do an audio or video interview with each older relative. Try to ask open ended questions, such as, "Grandma Johnson, tell me about where you grew up." "Uncle Fred, what do you remember about your grandfather, Bill Smith?" Avoid intimidating your subject or influencing their responses. Never assume you know the correct answer and that they might have forgotten it. Something that you thought was rock solid true, may turn out to be completely different once you complete your research. Try to get full names and complete dates when possible. Have them take you as far back as they can remember with the family tree.

Sometimes small things can be very important later. As an example, my grandmother vaguely remembered that her grandmother Mary Black, who died young, had a sister named Belle. After many years of research, I could confirm the correct family by finding a Belle and Mary on a census record as children in a family with a very common last name. Without this detail, it would have been very difficult to find the right family.

Don't take any piece of information for granted. Sometimes that is all you have to go on. Our ancestors had an interesting habit of naming their children after adult relatives. Thus, in one family you could find three Williams or Josephs all living in the same neighborhood. If the last name was common, it will just make your job more of a challenge.

Records and Photographs

While you are interviewing your subject, ask about any family photos they have of their past, especially of previous generations. Just seeing the photo can trigger additional recollections and names of great-aunts and great-uncles. Get copies of the photos and make notes of the names of the individuals. This may be a good time to invest in a portable scanner or digital camera to allow you to make an instant copy of the photo. Your relative might not want to let it leave the house, even to run down to the local copy shop! This also works well with other documents, such as birth and marriage certificates. A digital camera will allow you to view your work immediately to insure a good copy.

Survey the Landscape

If you are traveling away from home to interview your relatives, plan extra time to visit the local town to pick up more clues. Find out from your relative if any of your ancestors lived in the area. Visit the local library to see if they have any information on your family or local events that might have occurred while your family lived there. Examples include a Civil War battle, flood or another historic event.

Ask the librarian about local history books and biographies. Such books were very popular during the 19th century. You might find a biography on one of your relatives with three generations of family history, plus a picture of the original settler! Get as much information as possible to add to your background file. These events help to "fill in" the story of your ancestors and make their lives more complete. Look through copies of old newspapers, local history books and city directories for information on your family names.

Many libraries have printed indexes of county records such as birth, death and marriage. Check these for anyone with the same surname as that of your ancestors. Make copies of the indexes. If you find later that the list does contain related individuals, you can write the county for a copy of the actual record. (See Chapter 8, County Government Records, for more information).

See if the library has local cemetery records, such as burial or tombstone lists. They may even have mortuary records. Copy down any name like that of your ancestor's. If you have time, you might want to visit the cemetery and take a picture of the tombstones. If you are certain your ancestor once lived in town, use city directories to find their old home or business address. Drive by and see if the structure still stands. Take lots of pictures for your file.

What if your relative tells you none of your ancestors ever lived in town? Visit the library anyway. Every library has some genealogical materials. You may find a book written by some distant relative that has information on your family or a county history that is out of print and hard to find. Never judge a library by its size! I have found libraries in small towns may have more usable information than a large metropolitan library. Ask the librarian about your family name and if there are any books or records on that name. Check the local phone book for other individuals with that name. You may find they are related in some way.

Historical and genealogical societies are also a great source of information. Before your trip, see if one exists in the area you plan to visit. Determine the hours of operation. Many are staffed by volunteers and may only be open a few hours a week. See if you can get a general list of their holdings and special collections. Many times, local history materials such as county records, manuscripts, photographs and other materials will be donated to the society for safekeeping and preservation.

Chapter Action Plan

- Interview living relatives about their lives
- Ask about their parents and grandparents
- Get copies of photographs, bible records and other documents such as newspaper clippings, graduation announcements, marriage, death and bible records
- Visit the local library and research your target family names
- Make copies of promising indexes, biographies, city directories and other information
- Check cemetery records and visit ones with family names
- Photograph everything. Digital media is cheap and reusable!

Chapter 5
Organization, Organization, Organization

There are only two lasting bequests we can give our children
one is roots; the other, wings.
--Anonymous

Now that you have begun to gather data, photographs and other information, it is time to get organized so you don't get confused with all the names, dates and places you are collecting.

Pick Your Research Method
Decide how you will manage your materials so you can expand outside your immediate family. I recommend continuing with the file folder method begun in Chapter 3. With this approach, you will start a new file for each family (married couple plus their children). You will have a file for your parents, your grandparents (x2), and your great-grandparents (x4) and so on. Each file will contain documents, photographs and mementos for every member of that family, including children and spouses of children. As your file expands, you will replace it with a divided folder or accordion folder to separate the materials by child.

You will add a divider for each of the above families in your three-ring binder. Your completed research notes will be added here with a family group sheet and census log for each family (more about this later). The three-ring binder goes with you in the field as you visit relatives, libraries, court houses and other research locations. When your binder gets full, you may want to move your mother's ancestral line to a new binder.

The first binder will then contain only your father's line. As you complete (as much as anyone can) a specific family group, such as your grandparents, you might want to move all their research notes to your file folder for safe keeping. Retain their family group sheet in the binder.

Numbering Systems

As you add names to your file, you will soon find it difficult to keep track of who belongs in which family. Luckily, numbering systems have been developed to help reduce the confusion. The most basic is a system that identifies each generation beginning with you. You are number one. Number two is your father and number three is your mother. All males receive even numbers and all females receive odd numbers. This is the basic pedigree chart or family tree method. A pedigree chart shows direct line ancestors or progenitors from your mother and father, their father and mother, and so on. As stated earlier, a five-generation pedigree chart contains 31 individuals. This is a worthy goal for any beginning genealogist. (See illustration #5-1 for a sample pedigree chart)

Your beginning pedigree chart is labeled number 1. If you can take a family line beyond the first five generations, you would start a new chart. The number of the chart is determined by the number of the first person listed on the chart.

For example, person number 16 on chart number 1 is listed as the first person on chart number 2. Person number 17 on chart number 1 is listed as the first person on chart number 3, and so on. In the beginning, complete your charts by hand so you can get used to the system and understand the relationship between each generation. Once you have gathered several generations of information on several families, you might want to consider a genealogical software or spreadsheet program to help add and correct information to your database. (See the Chapter 14 for more information)

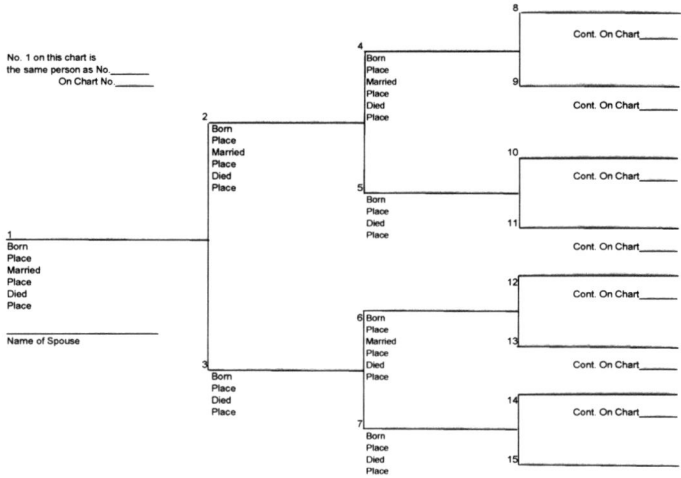

Illustration No. 5-1 Sample Pedigree Chart

Forms and Formats

We now know how to number the direct line ancestors, but how do we list children of those ancestors? The family group sheet (See Illustration #5-2) gives you a uniform method to gather family data. The parents are listed at the top of the page along with their vital information, such as date and place of birth, date and place of marriage and date and place of death. Additional information may include date and place of burial, baptism, confirmation, christening, parents' names and other spouses' names, if any.

Each child is listed, normally in birth order after the parents. With the child's full name, date and place of birth or christening, or both, date of death and place and marriage date and place with the name of spouse or spouses. To keep things straight, you may want to place an "x" or other mark next to the child that is your direct ancestor. As an example, on your maternal grandparent's family sheet, you would place an "x" next to your mother.

If a parent remarried and had additional children by the new spouse, a separate family group sheet should be prepared, even if your direct ancestor was not born in this family. The information you gather will help uncover new clues and possibly distant cousins you never knew you had. I have found these cousins to be very helpful in completing the full picture of your ancestor. Remember, they share that same ancestor with you and may have accumulated documents, family stories and heirlooms that you never knew existed!

As with the pedigree chart, start with yourself and complete your own family group sheet, then complete one for your parents, grandparents and one for each generation that you have found at least the names of the parents. You will now have a framework to complete additional research to fill in the gaps. I complete my initial family sheets with pencil until I know the information is accurate and provable.

At that time, I add it to my genealogical software program along with the source citations. I know now that if I print a family chart to share with others, it is as complete and accurate as possible and I will not be adding to the vast wasteland of undocumented family trees that are choking the Internet. The family group sheet is then added to your research binder to complete your "field manual". But before we get started, we need to establish a few rules and regulations.

Illustration No. 5-2 Sample Family Group Sheet

Family Names

Unless your ancestors were Native American, they immigrated to this country at some point in the past. There is a very good chance that their surname changed, either by choice or by accident. My immigrant ancestor's last name was Lang. He came from Germany or Switzerland and settled in Pennsylvania before the Revolutionary War. At some point, his children began using the surname Long. This may have been because the German pronunciation of Lang sounds likes "Long", or that the children wanted an "Americanized" name. Whatever the reason, my research in the U.S. involves the name of Long, but in Germany it will be Lang.

Many American family names were changed from their original European spellings. Schmidt became Smith, Muller became Miller, and Becker became Baker. These are just a few examples of the ways immigrate names were changed. Also, keep in mind, illiteracy was common and names were spelled phonetically, subject to the whims of the writer. Early documents, such as land, marriage and census records, might contain several variations of the same name, even in the same document. As you begin your research and look at indexes, rolls and databases, make a list of possible spelling variations. Don't assume that the name you are seeking is spelling exactly as expected. Humans created these records and humans are not perfect.

Date and Place Name Formats

Early in your research, you must develop methods to standardize the way you list dates and place names, both to reduce error and confusion and to help you find where your ancestors lived. Dates can be listed in many different formats. Does 4/3/01 mean April 3, 2001 or March 4th, 1801? To keep dates uniform in your research, always write them as DD MMM YYYY, such as 12

Dec 1945. Always list the full year, because you will be working with several different centuries, possibly even B.C.!

When you only have a partial date or date range, you need to list an estimated date, such as about 1832 or abt 1832. Some use c1832 or circa instead of about. If you have a date range, list it as 1828-1836 or "between 1828-1836". It is much better to list at least some date than to leave the date blank, so you can put this person in the proper time range and distinguish them from other individuals with the same name.

Because so many of the records we seek are located at the county level, it is important to always list the county name with the city, town or village, such as city, county, state, country. In Europe, it might be village, parish, county or shire, province or state, country. If you don't know the entire place name, use commas to illustrate what is missing, such as Tombstone, , Arizona, USA.

This tells you that you still need to find the county. If you get in the habit of listing all parts of the locale, you will avoid searching in the wrong place for your ancestors. Many states have both counties and towns with the same name.

If you are missing parts of a location, there are many resources to help you find it. Use maps, gazetteers, databases and other resources, including Global Positioning System (GPS) to find exact coordinates.

The history of the United States is one of expansion and change. Territories were created which were subdivided into states, then counties. County boundaries changed over time. Since many of the records you seek are held at the county level, it is important to find the right county for the period you are searching. As an example, if your ancestral family settled in the northeast corner of present day Houston County, Tennessee, and never moved, they would have seen the following changes:

1776 Washington District, North Carolina
1784 Washington District, Franklin
1789 Washington District, North Carolina
1790 Tennessee County, Southwest Territory
1796 Montgomery County, Tennessee
1803 Dickinson County, Tennessee
1871 Houston County, Tennessee

Always list the location as it was at the time of the event. If your ancestor was born in 1790 in present day Houston County, Tennessee, list the place name as Tennessee County, Southwest Territory. Since records are kept at the county level in existence at the time of the event, it is important to find the proper repository. You may end up searching more than one to find the desired record.

Two excellent resources to aid in finding the correct jurisdiction include **The International Vital Records Handbook** by Thomas Kemp and **Map Guide to the U.S. Federal Censuses, 1790-1920,** by William Thorndale and William Dollarhide, both available through Genealogical Publishing Co, *http://www.genealogical.com/*

Chapter Action Plan

- Choose a method to organize your materials and data
- Begin completing family group sheets and pedigree charts
- Make a list of various spellings of each family surname in your research list
- Use proper date and place name conventions
- Make a list of counties your ancestors lived, including the county seat

Chapter 6
The Local Library

Genealogists live in the past lane
--Unknown

A great place to start your serious research is at the local library. Call ahead to see what genealogical materials and support they offer. Some libraries have a separate genealogical department staffed with knowledgeable genealogists who can help you find the right resources for your search.

Others have at least several stacks of books on local, county and state history, genealogical reference materials and even microfilm readers and/or computers linked to the Internet to help with your research.

Library Resources and Guidance
After locating the closest library with the best resources, plan to spend the day taking a tour of the department, getting to know what is available and where best to start your research. Tap into the experience and knowledge of the staff to help guide you. Remember, they have probably been asked the following question at least 500 times before, "Can you help me find my ancestor who fought in the Civil War?" Some libraries have volunteer staffers from the local genealogical or historical society that can help as well.

Don't be overwhelmed by the large amount of materials. Look at the card catalog to see how they group records. Many libraries have a subject index listed by state and county, with all materials related to that county filed together. See if your library has a computerized card catalog that can be searched by subject. This allows you to create a list of potential resources you would like to view. Once you have your list with reference numbers, ask the librarian how you locate the materials. If the computerized card catalog is available online you can create your list at home and then take it with you to the library, saving you precious research time.

Keep focused on your family, starting with the most recent members and moving back in time as you document the data. Most libraries with genealogical departments offer the following resources:

- Local Histories and Biographies
- City Directories & Telephone Books
- Newspaper Archives
- County Birth, Death & Marriage Indexes
- Genealogical & Historical Periodicals
- Microfilm Census Records

- Printed Census Indexes
- Military Service and Pension Records
- Property Tax Records

Target Your Research

Ask the librarian to help you with a specific problem. Say you want to find the name of the parents of your great-grandmother, Mary, who married Tom Smith. You don't know her maiden name. The librarian will lead you through a series of steps to identify records that might help you find the answer in the shortest period. If you know where Tom & Mary lived after their marriage, you may be directed to county marriage records to see if they were also married there.

Check surrounding counties. Your goal is to find Mary's maiden name and then work to find her parents. Families who lived in the same communities often inter-married and moved westward together. If you can find Tom & Mary on a census record, perhaps her parents lived close by or, as they aged, may have lived in Tom and Mary's household. Census records will be covered in detail in Chapter 9.

Microfilm and Microform Records

These technologies allow a huge amount of information to be stored in a small amount of space. Most libraries have microfilm and microfiche readers to allow you to access their records. Many census, tax, vital, probate, military, passenger list and county history records have been microfilmed and distributed to local libraries. You can come and spend hours viewing thousands of records that would normally take several hundred rows of storage in printed form.

Using these records requires patience and good eyesight. You must look through hundreds of sometimes faded, scratched microfilm copies of faded, damaged, hand-written documents. But when you find your family, it is all worth it! Most libraries also provide a microfilm copy machine, where you can make a paper copy of the pages with your family information. This provides a record for your file and provides a great place to site the source.

Interlibrary Loan

Even if your local library has a limited collection of genealogical books, you can access millions of resources through interlibrary loan. Your library can request books and other materials from the largest U.S. libraries, such as the New York Public Library, the Los Angeles Public Library, or the Fort Wayne Public Library, which has one of the largest genealogical collections in the county. Most large libraries have an on-line card catalog which lists their holdings. If you find a book that might provide the information you need, you will be able request a copy to be sent to your local library for your review. And it's usually free!

Computerized Resources

Many libraries now offer personal computers with access to on-line databases. These include census indexes, vital records indexes, passenger lists, church records, family tree submissions, military records and much more. The two most common are Heritage Quest and Ancestry.com, which provide quick access to millions of records. This can save you time by quickly searching large amounts of data in a short period. Ask your librarian to explain these services, how you access them and if there are any time limits imposed on your research. Most computers are attached to a printer which allows you to print potential matches of your family. This makes a great addition to your research folder to help you document what has been researched. It also gives you the information necessary to request a copy of the original document.

Chapter Action Plan

- Survey the area for local libraries with genealogical collections
- Plan a day-long trip to the selected library to learn about their collections, resources and staff
- Ask the librarian specific questions to help narrow your research focus
- Look for county records collections and develop a list of materials to be researched
- Keep good records of what has been searched, and include the source for all information you collect
- See what digital and on-line databases are available to aid in your search
- Use interlibrary loan to research books not found locally

Chapter 7
Documenting Your Sources

Those who forget their past are destined to repeat it
-- Robert A. Heinlein

In your research, you stumble across a long-lost cousin who has produced a family tree back to the 16th century. He offers to send you a copy to help in your research. You receive the material and find that there are no sources cited for the data provided. What do you do?

Aunt Martha Told Me So
As stated in the interview section, take all information you receive with a degree of skepticism. You must find your own proof to substantiate the information. Family trees with no documentation are not worth the paper they are printed on. To answer the above question, use your cousin's material as a springboard to additional research. Never assume it is correct until you have provided the appropriate evidence.

Proper Research Methods
Standards for Sound Genealogical Research
Recommended by the National Genealogical Society

Remembering always that they are engaged in a quest for truth, family history researchers consistently

Record the source for each item of information they collect
Test every hypothesis of theory against credible evidence, and reject those that are not supported by the evidence
Seek original records, or reproduced images of them when there is reasonable assurance they have not been altered, as the basis for their research conclusions
Use compilations, communications and published works, whether paper or electronic, primarily for their value as guides to locating the original records, or as contributions to the critical analysis of the evidence discussed in them
State something as a fact only when it is supported by convincing evidence, and identify the evidence when communicating the fact to others
Limit with words like "probable" or "possible" any statement that is based on less than convincing evidence, and state the reasons for concluding that it is probable or possible
Avoid misleading other researchers by either intentionally or carelessly distributing or publishing inaccurate information
State carefully and honestly the results of their own research, and acknowledge all use of other researchers' work
Recognize the collegial nature of genealogical research by making their work available to others through publication, or by placing copies in appropriate libraries or repositories, and by welcoming critical comment

Consider with open minds new evidence of the comments of others on their work and the conclusions they have reached

© 1997, 2002 by National Genealogical Society. *Permission is granted to copy or publish this material provided it is reproduced in its entirety, including this notice.*

Source Citations

Get in the habit of citing your sources whether you are at the library taking notes, making copies of materials or at home adding data to your computer. Your computer program will probably allow you to add comments and even an image of the source to your citation. This allows you or any future researcher to go back to the original source to verify the information, or maybe add to what has already been done. An excellent guide to source citation is Elizabeth Shown Mills, **Evidence! Citation & Analysis for the Family Historian**, available from Amazon, *http://www.amazon.com*.

Her book lists many examples of the proper way to list source citations that are attached to family history data. Samples are given for listing books, periodicals, birth records, marriage records, deeds, thesis, town records, emails, electronic files and many other sources. She discusses tracking sources in two distinct ways,

"A bibliography is an abbreviated reference tool – a nonspecific "master list" for quick consultation. It does not document any particular fact. Its primary purpose during research is to keep track of the materials you have examined. Its function in a published work is to provide the reader with a convenient summary of the relevant resources."

"Individual source notes – with complete and specific reference data – should be used when transcribing documents, making abstracts, photocopying materials, preparing research reports (for our own files or for others) and writing family accounts".

Here are a few examples of correct source citation for a short section of text:

John Lonass (Lonas) was born about 1759 in Germany.[1] On 16 February 1779 he married Mary Keplinger in Frederick, Frederick, Maryland.[2] John entered service in the German Regiment of the State of Maryland in the War of the Revolution and died while on duty on 2 October 1782.[3]

---

[1] John Lonass file, no W19252, Revolutionary War Pension Applications (Washington: National Archives)

[2] John Louis (sp) and Mary Keplinger Marriage License dated 16 February 1779, Clerk of the Circuit Court's Office, Frederick, Frederick, Maryland.

[3] *Muster Rolls of Maryland Troops in the American Revolution, 1775-1783*, (Baltimore: Genealogical Publishing Company, 1972).

Internet GEDCOM

GEDCOM is an acronym for Genealogical Data Communication; it's a method of formatting the text of your family data so that different software programs and operating systems can read and understand it. GEDCOMS were developed to allow researchers to share files with other researchers who used non-compatible software programs. It's like a universal language translator for genealogical software.

The Internet allows this transfer of files to happen on an enormous scale. Many websites support GEDCOM uploads so others can download into their own program. Unfortunately, the clear majority of these files contain un-documented conclusions. Once on the web, the information is taken as gospel and re-circulated many times over.

If you find a GEDCOM file with information that might pertain to your family be very cautious about the contents. If you decide to download the file, keep it separate from your own research until each date, place and claim can be verified independently. If you casually add the file to your own, you may find you cannot remember what has been documented and what has not, causing many hours of backtracking. Beware!

Chapter Action Plan

- Follow proper research methods
- Document all sources using established standards
- Get documentation information at the time you collect the data, as it will be much harder to re-trace your steps later
- Add source citations to your genealogy program or other data gathering program
- Be wary of GEDCOM files that contain undocumented information

Chapter 8
County Government Records

Everyone has ancestors and it is only a question of going back far enough to find a good one
--Howard Kenneth Nixon

Now that you have found some clues about your ancestors, it is time to begin searching for primary sources. These include court records, church records, wills, letters, autobiographies and any other record that was created at the time of the event. They are first-hand accounts acquired through direct experience.

Secondary sources are comments or interpretations of primary sources. These include newspaper accounts, biographies, obituaries, compilations of records from other sources, and second-hand accounts of past events or dates.

You will want to focus on primary sources for your research, using secondary sources as backup or background research.

Where to Start Looking

As you complete your family tree chart and family group sheets, you will list where your ancestors were born, married and died. You will list the city and county name. From this you will find the county seat and the county court house where records are kept. Before you plan a trip to the court house, or send a letter, check to see of county records indexes can be found at your local library or on the web. What records can be found at the county level?

Birth Records

Most counties began keeping birth records at some time in their existence. Generally, in the early 20th century, this responsibility was transferred to the state government. If you ancestor was born after 1900, check with the state department of health (or similar office) to see if their record is available.

You can find a list of state vital records offices at http://www.cdc.gov/nchs/howto/w2w/w2welcom.htm.

If your ancestor was born before 1900, check to see if the county kept birth records for that period. It varies widely from county to county and state to state. Additionally, many New England states required the town clerks to record births. Outside of New England, the recording of births was incomplete and mainly occurred after 1880.

Early birth records primarily recorded the name of the child, the names of the parents and the date of birth. In some cases, not even the child's name is listed, only male or female. Later records include the place of birth, place of residence, name of informant and attending physician.

If you find an index or other source that leads you to believe your ancestor's birth record may be on file at a county court house, you must write and ask for a copy. In some cases, you can send the letter and ask that they bill you for the fees. Other counties will require payment before you get your copy. It is important to determine the proper department to send your request. Depending on the county, it could be the county clerk, the probate clerk, the county auditor, the register of deeds, or other offices. To find the right address and office check the county's website.

Marriage Records

As with birth records, marriage records were maintained sporadically, except for New England until the early 18th century. As counties were formed during the westward expansion, most clerks began keeping marriage returns. As with birth, you must determine where your ancestors may have been married and determine if a record exists. Since they were not required to obtain a marriage license in their native county, you should check records of surrounding counties as well.

When dealing with marriage records, terminology is important. The following types of marriage records will help you with your research:

Marriage License – issued by a county or town authorizing a marriage upon application and payment of fee. Generally, includes the names of the bride and groom, the date and place of issuance and the name of the official. In some cases, it might include additional information such as ages, dates of birth and address of the bride and groom, plus their parent's names.

Marriage Return – Once the marriage was completed by a minister, justice of the peace or other official, it was returned with the date of the marriage and the signature and title of the officiator. Many returns were never completed.

Marriage Bann - A public proclamation of a couple's intent to marry, a bann is an ecclesiastical custom several centuries old. It gives the public an opportunity to come forward with reasons for the marriage not to occur. Normally found in church records.

Marriage Intention – Like a marriage bann published by a church, this was recorded in town meeting books prior to the marriage.

Marriage Bond – This is found primarily in Southern states. It affirmed that there was no moral or legal reason why the couple could not be married. A financial amount deposited generally by the groom's relatives to offset any legal action if the couple could not be married. Many times, the bondsman was the father of the groom or another close relative of the groom. The name of the bride and groom, date and place of issue and the name of the bondsman or surety were listed. The bond was not evidence of marriage and was generally issued before the marriage took place.

Marriage records are important for genealogical research, because they provide a place and date of marriage and list the full name of the bride. This may lead to finding the parents of the bride and locating other relatives of both the bride and groom. Because many families lived on isolated farms, individuals tended to marry neighbors or members of their church.

When viewing count y or town marriage indexes, also look for other individuals with the same last name as your ancestors'. You may later find a relationship exists. Make copies of the indexes and keep them in your folders. It may save you another trip back to the library or archive.

Death Records

Death records were sporadic, but if maintained are generally found at the county or town level until the early 20th century. As with birth, the state took this responsibility beginning around 1900. If you find a county death record for your ancestor, it will probably contain the name of the deceased, date and cause of death and name of spouse or parents. Some city health departments kept these records to track potential outbreaks of infectious disease, such as yellow fever, influenza, cholera, scarlet fever and other ailments. If you can't find a state or county death record, always check for a city record.

Probate Records

When your ancestor died, their estate was settled through the probate process. It is helpful to know important terms:

Testate – dying with a will. The executor named in the will files a petition for probate. Normally a bond is posted by the executor and witnesses are called to testify about the testator's state of mind and body at the time the will was written.

Intestate – dying without a will. Letters of administration are filed by the next of kin or surviving spouse and a hearing is held to name the administrator. A bond is posted by the administrator.

Inventory – a list of all personal and real property of the decedent.

Appointments of guardian – issued when the decedent had minor children.

Decree of distributions – lists those who receive distributions of estate assets and sometimes their relationship to the decedent.

If you ancestor left a will, it provides family relationships, such as spouse, children and grandchildren. If a child of the decedent pre-deceased the decedent, the grandchildren may receive the portion that would have gone to the child.

Take the estate of John Jones, whose will read: ...and to my granddaughter Mary Smith, the sum of ten dollars I formerly willed to my deceased daughter Elizabeth Smith. This helps to not only confirm that Elizabeth is the daughter of the decedent, but that her married name is Smith and she died before the will of John Jones was written. Additionally, it establishes a relationship between Elizabeth Smith and Mary Smith which may help complete the family group sheet for Elizabeth.

Even if your ancestor did not leave a will, the final distribution and inventory might tell you the spouse, children, grandchildren, spouses of children and close friends of the decedent. This can be valuable material for tying the family together with other information.

Probate records can be found in published indexes or abstracts, microfilmed records and on-line indexes. Once you find your ancestor's estate was probated in a particular county, write to the appropriate clerk in that county for a copy of the will and full probate file. It may be a large file and expensive to copy, but it could help you find that elusive clue you are looking for.

Land records

Land was a valuable asset for our ancestors because most of them farmed and the land provided the resource needed to make a living. From colonial times land was granted for cash, service and to encourage settlement. States provided bounty lands to Revolutionary soldiers for their service. Many took the offer and moved west to receive the bounty warrant or another grant.

A **deed** provides the instrument to transfer title to property from one party to another. A **grantor** (seller) would transfer ownership to the **grantee** (buyer) as a gift or in exchange for money or other property. Deed books have two primary indexes, the grantor and grantee index. While researching your ancestor, you should look at both. Try locating all transactions involving your ancestor both as grantee and grantor. The first time your ancestor appears in deed records should be as grantee or buyer of property in the county. If your ancestor moved on to another county, the last entry should be as grantor, or seller.

Many times, the land will be transferred through deed of gift to a child. This will provide a connection between parent and child. Deeds of gift were also used to transfer land ownership to a daughter upon her marriage. This document could provide evidence of marriage, identify the bride's parents and confirm her maiden name. Other land transactions might help identify family friends, neighbors and in-laws. This provides you clues to follow in additional records.

Any deed records you find should be abstracted and added to your family file. The following information should be included in your abstract:

- Date of the deed and date it was filed
- grantors and grantees and residence
- type of deed
- full description of the property
- price paid and any other consideration
- witnesses and signatures or marks
- any relationships stated and names of other individuals listed
- volume, page number and county where filed

Courthouse Etiquette

If you visit the county courthouse in person, come prepared and act professionally as you visit each clerk's office. Bring a typewritten list with the following information: your ancestors' full name, the type of record you seek, such as death, probate, marriage, and the approximate date of the event. Go to the appropriate department that may hold the record and ask the clerk if you can view the index for the period you seek.

The clerk will, either take you to the record room and allow you to look through the index, or look through the index for you. If you find a potential match, right down every piece of information, such as the names listed, dates, volume or book number, page number or record number. This will allow you to find the actual record in the original book or file. In larger counties, the records may have been digitized or microfilmed to preserve old documents and to provide access to a larger number of researchers.

Remember, the clerks are not employed by the county to do genealogical research for you, so you must know what your objectives are and whether the courthouse might offer you a solution. Once you find the original record, read it carefully to see if it involves your ancestor. Indexes are often wrong and the record may be in another book or on another page.

Read all the names in the record to see if you should expand your index research to cover new potential connections. Write a brief abstract of the record, including type of record, date and names. Ask for a copy. The clerk may be able to remove the page from the binder and make a photo copy, or require it be sent somewhere else in the building for copying. It may not be possible to receive the copy before you leave, so have the copy mailed to you. For this reason, you should bring along a few self-addressed stamped envelopes. This will speed up the process and will be appreciated by the clerk. Have cash or a check handy to pay for copies and other services.

Before completing your visit, ask if there are any records in the office that may be of interest to a family researcher for the period of your study. You may find that they have local or state census records, tax records, voting records, plat books or other records that can add to your family file and help locate where your ancestor lived. If you traveled to visit the courthouse, plan enough extra time to visit the local library.

Additional Resources

Land & Property Research in the United States, E. Wade Hone, Salt Lake City, UT: Ancestry, 1997. *https://www.amazon.com/*

How to Read Probate Records,
http://www.dohistory.org/on_your_own/toolkit/probateRecords.html

Locating Your Roots: Discover Your Ancestors Using Land Records, Patricia Law Hatcher, Cincinnati, OH: Betterway Books, 2003. *https://www.amazon.com/*

Chapter Action Plan

- Determine what records may exist at the county level
- Find the county seat and address to write for additional information
- Determine the appropriate county office that may hold the records you seek
- Check on-line resources, county records indexes and other resources to see if you can find your ancestor in the indexes
- Write to or visit the courthouse in person to locate and copy needed documents
- After adding the information to your database, properly cite the sources
- Keep copies of records and abstracts in your family file

Chapter 9
National Archives Records
Census

The more I study my family tree, the less census it makes!
--Anonymous

The National Archives and Records Administration (NARA) is an independent Federal agency that preserves our nation's history and defines us as a people by overseeing the management of all Federal records. The Archives provide a wealth of genealogical materials. The Archives are in Washington, DC, but 11 regional centers are scattered throughout the country.

These regional sites allow researchers access to many of the same materials located in Washington. The book, Guide to Genealogical Research in the National Archives. Washington, DC: National Archives and Records Administration, 3d edition, 2001., provides an overview of records you will probably work with most often. Available from the National Archives at 1-800-234-8861 or on-line at: *http://www.archives.gov/*

Many records are incomplete and may have been damaged over time. The 1890 US census was almost completely lost in a fire in 1921. Many of the record sets are available on microfilm at many larger U.S. libraries and the regional archives centers. They can also be ordered from the National Archives and from the Family History Library in Salt Lake City.

What Do Census Records Offer Me?

Census records contain the name of every head of household in the US at the time of the decennial census. Of course, not everyone was counted, just as often happens in modern census returns, but a good majority of the population was included. The amount of information collected was expanded with each succeeding census. Census returns are released only after a period of 72 years, so we have 1790 through 1940 available as of this writing. Most major libraries have most if not all the current returns and indexes on microfilm. If your local library does not, you can order microfilm rolls through interlibrary loan, visit the National Archives in Washington, or a regional center, or request rolls through a local Family History Center. See the following link for locations:

http://www.familysearch.org/Eng/Library/FHC/frameset_fhc.asp?PAGE=library_fhc_find.asp

Most census records have now been digitized and are available through an on-line subscription service at Ancestry, *http://www.ancestry.com*. FamilySearch.com now has most census records available on-line for free.

1790-1840
The first five federal census schedules only provide basic information, such as the name of the head of the household and the number of additional individuals by age, sex and race. The heads of the household are listed by State, County, Township or other subdivision.

The 1790 census index has been published for all existing schedules. Returns for Delaware, Georgia, Kentucky, New Jersey, Tennessee and Virginia were destroyed by fire, apparently during the War of 1812. The Virginia census has been reproduced using state enumerations.

The 1800-1840 schedules have been microfilmed and indexed. If you know which state your ancestor resided during the census year, you can find them on a statewide index, then locate them on the appropriate roll of microfilm containing the county they resided.

1850-1940
The 1850 schedule is the first to list all household members by name, age, sex and relationship to the head of the household. Many times, you can find multiple generations living in the same household. This provides a way to confirm relationships and develop leads for further research. Many related families lived close to each other and can be found by expanding your search beyond the target family. If you know your female ancestor's maiden name, you may be able to find her parents living close by in the same county. The 1890 US census was almost completely lost in a fire in 1921.

Where Can I Find Census Records?
National Archives and Record Administration, Washington, DC
http://www.nara.gov/
Region Records Centers (a list of regional centers can be found at: http://www.nara.gov/)
Local Library
FamilySearch.org
http://www.familysearch.org/

Using the Records
To complete a thorough search of census records, you must use the right tools. Each census schedule used a slightly different format as to the form and content of data collected. If you plan on viewing many census records, it is a good idea to have a guide listing the records and the information contained in each schedule.

Excellent guides include, **The 1790-1890 Federal Population Censuses: Catalog of National Archives Microfilm** (Washington, DC: National Archives Trust Fund Board, 1993). There is also a separate guide available from the National Archives for each census from 1900 to 1940.

Once you have an idea what records are available for your search and you know where to locate them, assemble the forms you will need:

Blank census forms (see Illustration No. 9-1)

Illustration No. 9-1 Sample Census Form

Finding Your Ancestor on the Census

Before spending hours of potentially fruitless searching, a little preparation can greatly enhance your potential for success. Use the following steps:

Create a list of the families you are trying to locate including the parent's names, children's names and approximate ages at the time of the census. Next to the parents' names, list all the possible locations they may have lived at the time of the census. Include town, township or city, county and state, if you have that information.

In searching, look for spelling variations and name abbreviations such as the following for the name "Joseph Thomas":

J. Thomas	J. Tomas
Jos Thomas	J. Thoms
Joe Thomas	J. Thomes
J.F. Thomas	J. Thommas

Remember, the census takers may not have asked exactly how to spell the name, or may have spelled it phonetically, or had poor handwriting so the index coders may not have read it correctly.

If you find you ancestor, write down all the information listed, including the city, town, county, enumeration district, supervisor's district, page number, family or dwelling number, line number, etc

Include the two families before and the two families after your family. If you are not 100% sure of the handwriting, list your interpretation and make a note next to the name indicating you are not sure of the exact spelling, etc.

Proper Census Research Methods

Do not use your previous research to jump to conclusions about a name or a person's age, place of birth, etc. Many times, the information given by the same person from census year to census year may not match up. You would expect them to age 10 years between enumerations, but that may not be what they tell the census taker, or the census taker wrote it down wrong. Additionally, the place of birth listed for a parent may not be consistent from year to year. Take the data down as you find it and build your conclusions later as you gather more resources.

Before you begin searching another census record, page through the township or enumeration district of your ancestor to locate other families with the same last name. Include in your search the related family names, such as in-laws, names found on wills, in county biographical records or other sources. You might stumble across brothers, sisters, or even parents and grandparents of your target family and related families. If you find potential candidates, add them to your census forms. Even if they prove later to be no connection, you will have information that you will not have to try to find later.

Lastly, make sure you write down enough information to properly list the census record as a source. The correct format for the 1900 census record from Smith County, Tennessee would be as follows:

[1.]Joseph Thomas household, 1900 U.S. census, Smith County, Tennessee, population schedule, town of Riddleton, enumeration district (ED) 231, supervisor's district (SD) 3, sheet 14, dwelling 153, family 173, National Archives micro-publication T623, roll 1600.

If you cannot locate your ancestor on the census index, and you know with some certainty that they lived in that state during that period, consider the following:

- The surname was seriously misspelled by either the census taker or the index compiler and it is filled under that misspelled name.
- Your ancestor was missed by the census taker.
- The original census returns for your ancestor's residence were either lost or destroyed.

Mortality Schedules

A separate census schedule was commissioned by Congress to collect data about persons who died during the census year. The first mortality census was completed in 1850. Additional schedules included 1860, 1870, 1880 and the limited 1885 census of Colorado, Dakota Territory, Florida, Nebraska and New Mexico Territory. Since the data only included one year out of ten, the number of deaths covered was very limited. Additionally, some of the returns have been lost over time. However, if you have an ancestor who died during the census year, they may appear on a mortality schedule. Information includes:
- Name of person
- Age
- Sex
- State of birth
- Month and cause of death
- State of birth of each parent (1880 and 1885 only)

Most schedules have been microfilmed and are available from the same repositories that hold regular census schedules.

State Census Records

Many states ran their own census enumerations or tax lists. These can be valuable tools in locating your ancestor and filling in the gaps between federal returns. Availability will vary from state to state, but many have been microfilmed, published or are available through electronic means.

An excellent resource for state census records is the US Census Bureau: https://www.census.gov/history/www/genealogy/other_resources/state_censuses.html

Analyzing Census Data

Once you have located your ancestor's family in several successive census schedules, you will have a lot of data to help you determine the parents' ages, children's sex, age range and other information. If your family lived primarily before 1850, this may be one of the only ways to determine this information. We will examine a family over several decades to narrow down ages and the number of children in each family. The census returns for the years 1790-1840 include only the head of the household by name. Other members are listed by sex and age range.

Remember, the census date was the official date of the census, but the enumerator could have visited the family several months before or after that date. As an example, the 1800 census was to begin on the first Monday in August 1800 and ended within 9 months. The 1830 census was to begin on June 1, 1830 and end within 6 months. The date the enumerator actually took the census data is listed at the top of the page of each census schedule. Keep these dates in mind when calculating potential birth dates.

The following family census summary of the Jonas Lindale family was compiled from census returns, 1790-1840. (See sample census analysis form, illustration 9-2)

Male/Female	1790	1800	1810	1820	1830	1840	Birth Range
Jonas	16+ b. by 1774	26-44 1755-1774	26-44 1765-1784	45+ b. by 1775	60-69 1760-1770	70-79 1760-1770	1765-1770
Wife		26-44 1755-1774	26-44 1765-1784	45+ b. by 1775	60-69 1760-1770	70-79 1760-1770	1765-1770
Male		0-9 1790-1800	16-25 1784-1794	26-44 1775-1794			1790-1794
Female		0-9 1790-1800	16-25 1784-1794	26-44 1775-1794			1790-1794
Male			10-15 1794-1800	18-25 1794-1801			1800

Illustration No. 9-2 Sample Census Analysis Form

Notice that the age ranges from each census help you narrow down the age range to a few years and sometimes to one year. Subsequent census returns and other documentation can confirm your hypothesis. This also helps eliminate other families with similar names in the same region.

For example: assume there was another Jonas Lindale family living in the same county and you were not sure which was the correct Jonas, father of your target ancestor. With this analysis, you can eliminate one Jonas perhaps because the number, sex or age of children in his family would not match your knowledge of your ancestor's family makeup.

Chapter Action Plan

- Review the types of census records that might help you find your ancestors
- Make a list of the states and census years for each family you are researching
- Maintain a log of all potential census records you wish to search to determine if it contains your target family
- When a family is found on a census return, record all information on a blank census form, including neighbors

Chapter 10
National Archives Records
Immigration and Naturalization

There is no king who has not had a slave among his ancestors,
and no slave who has not had a king among his
-- Helen Keller

Immigration Records (Ship Passenger Arrival Records)
Passenger arrival lists found in the National Archives record names of passengers arriving from abroad at ports on the Atlantic Ocean or the Gulf of Mexico and a few inland ports. Although there are lists as early as 1798, most cover the years 1820-1959, with many gaps in the records. San Francisco passenger lists were destroyed by fires in 1851 and 1940. Lists for other Pacific coast ports have not been transferred to the National Archives. The Archives has some records for the port of New Orleans and the port of Philadelphia prior to 1820.

The lists consist of customs passenger lists, customs list of aliens, and immigration passenger lists. The original lists were prepared on board ship by the captain of the vessel and filed later with the collector of customs when the ship reached port. Most lists contain the following information:

- Name of vessel
- Master of vessel
- Port of embarkation
- Date and port of arrival
- Passenger's name
- Passenger's age and sex
- Passenger's occupation
- Name of country or countries from which he/she came
- Country to which he/she was going

Finding records before 1820
The Archives does not maintain earlier records, but those that exist can be found in several collections that are located at most larger libraries and other repositories:

Filby, William, ed. **Passenger and Immigration Lists Index: A Guide to Published Records of Passengers Who Came to the United States and Canada in the Seventeenth, Eighteenth, and Nineteenth Centuries,** 3 volumes plus supplements. Detroit: Gale Research Co., 1981.

Filby, William, ed. **Passenger and Immigration Lists Bibliography, 1538-1900.** 2nd ed. Detroit: Gale Research Co., 1988

Lancour, Harold, comp. **A Bibliography of Ship Passenger Lists, 1538-1825; Being a Guide to Published Lists of Early Immigrants to North America**. 3rd ed. New York: New York Public Library, 1978.

Additionally, there have been many compilations of lists made over the years to help fill in the gaps. These can also be found at major repositories.

Accessing the records at the National Archives

Researchers can search the records at the National Archives in Washington, DC. The Regional Records Centers have selected immigration records, but researchers are urged to call ahead to confirm the records availability. Many large libraries have obtained all or part of the microfilm rolls of passenger records. You can also obtain records by sending Form 81 to the Archives. You must provide the full name of the passenger, port of entry, and approximate date of arrival. Archives personnel will search the following indexes to determine if your ancestor can be located:

- Baltimore (1820-1952)
- Boston (1848-1891 and 1902-1920)
- New Orleans (1853-1952)
- New York (1820-1846 and 1897-1948)
- Philadelphia (1800-1948)
- Some Minor Ports (1820-1874 and 1890-1924)

The Archives cannot search un-indexed records without also having the name of the vessel. Form 81 can be obtained from the National Archives at: *http://www.nara.gov/*. If your ancestor is found, a copy of the passenger list containing your ancestor will be sent to you in exchange for a fee. If the search is unsuccessful, you will not be charged.

On-line Passenger Lists

As with census records, passenger lists are being digitized to allow on-line research. The following collection provides access to records for a fee: Ancestry.com at: *http://ancestry.com/*.

Naturalization Records

Naturalization records captured the timeline of events wherein an immigrant to the United States declared his or her intention of becoming a full-fledged citizen. As a rule, naturalization was a two-step process that took a minimum of 5 years. After residing in the United States for 2 years, an alien could file a "declaration of intent" to become a citizen. After 3 additional years, the alien could "petition for naturalization." After the petition was granted, a certificate of citizenship was issued to the alien. The declaration of intent generally contains more genealogically useful information.

The alien could become naturalized in any court of record, including county, state and federal courts. Most applicants filed at the county level because that was the most easily accessible. These courts can include supreme, circuit, district, equity, chancery, probate, or common pleas. Today these records may still be held at the county court, in a county or State archives or regional archives. As a rule, the National Archives does not have naturalization records created in State or local courts, however, some county records have been donated to the Archives.

If the naturalization took place in a Federal court, naturalization indexes, declarations of intent, and petitions will usually be found in the NARA regional facility serving the State in which the Federal court is located.

Naturalization applications typically included the applicant's name, age, place and date of birth, allegiance, and the date of the declaration. After 1866, the forms usually offered a physical description (including height, weight, eye color, complexion, and identifying marks), a current place of residence, last foreign address, the name of the ship, and the port and date of entry.

National Archives Collections

The National Archives has copies of naturalization papers (1798 – 1906) for Massachusetts, New Hampshire, Rhode Island and Maine and original records (1802-1926) for the District of Columbia. For records after September 26, 1906, contact the Immigration and Naturalization Service (Now called the U.S. Citizenship & Immigration Services), Washington, DC 20536. http://www.uscis.gov/

Additional Resources:

Christina K. Schaefer, **Guide to Naturalization Records of the United States** (Baltimore: Genealogical Publishing Co., 1997).

John J. Newman, **American Naturalization Processes and Procedures, 1790-1985**. Published by the Family History Section of the Indiana Historical Society in 1985, it has been revised and expanded as American Naturalization Records, 1790-1990 (Bountiful, Utah: Heritage Quest, 1998.)

Loretto Dennis Szucs, **They Became Americans: Finding Naturalization Records and Ethnic Origins** (Salt Lake City: Ancestry, 1998).

The Family History Library has the largest collection of naturalization records in print and on microfilm. You can access their collection by visiting the main library in Salt Lake City or on-line. For more information visit *http://familysearch.org/*

Additional On-line Naturalization Resources

Ancestry.com includes naturalization records as part of their immigration records collection. More information can be obtained at *http://www.ancestry.com/*

Chapter Action Plan
- If you have ancestors that arrived in U.S. ports after 1820, determine if passenger lists may exist in the National Archives or on-line
- Obtain copies if possible of all potential passenger lists
- Determine where your ancestor may have applied for citizenship and check court records
- Check on-line resources and other databases for additional information

Chapter 11
National Archives Records
Military

Friends come and go, but relatives tend to accumulate
--Anonymous

Records Collections – Washington & St. Louis
Military and pension records can provide a wealth of information on your ancestor and his family. Records are maintained at two primary facilities: The National Archives Building in Washington, D.C. and the National Personnel Records Center (NPRC) in St. Louis, MO. The records for military service before WWI are generally held in Washington, D.C., while later records are held in St. Louis.

National Archives in Washington:

Branch of Service	Dates
Volunteers	Persons serving during an emergency whose service was in the Federal Interest, 1775-1902
Regular Army	Enlisted personnel, 1789-October 31, 1912 Officers, 1789-June30, 1917
Navy	Enlisted personnel, 1789-1904 Some officers, 1789-1895
Marine Corps	Enlisted personnel, 1789-1904 Some officers, 1789-1895
Coast Guard	Individuals who served in predecessor agencies, such as the Revenue Cutter Service, the Life-Saving Service and the Lighthouse Service, 1791-1919
Confederate States	Military service rendered for the Confederate States government, 1861-1865
Veterans Records	Claims files for pensions based on Federal military service, 1775-1916 and Bounty land warrant application files relating to claims based on wartime service, 1775-1855

Records held in St. Louis:

Branch of Service	Dates
U.S. Army	Officers separated after June 29, 1917 Enlisted personnel separated after October 31, 1912 Note: Many records were destroyed by fire in the St. Louis Center in 1973.
U.S. Air Force	Officers and enlisted personnel separated after September 24, 1947

U.S. Navy	Officers separated after 1901
	Enlisted personnel separated after 1884
U.S. Marine Corps	Officers separated after 1904
	Enlisted personnel separated after 1905
U.S. Coast Guard	Officers separated after 1897
	Enlisted personnel separated after 1905
U.S. Coast Guard predecessor agencies	Civilian employees of agencies such as Revenue Cutter Service, Lifesaving Service, and Lighthouse Service, retired after 1919

To access these records, you must first determine if your ancestor did serve in a branch of the service during the time periods covered by the records. You will also need information, such the regiment, or unit name, state from which he served and file number or pension application number. If he served in the Civil War, you need to know whether he was Union or Confederate.

Researching the Available Records

Begin your research by consulting the appropriate name indexes found on National Archives microfilm. These index cards are arranged alphabetically by surname and show the soldier's name, rank, and the unit or units in which he served. There are also cross-references to names that appear in the records under various spellings. Consult the National Archives' **Microfilm Resources for Research: A Comprehensive Catalog** (2000) for a list of microfilmed name indexes and compiled service records. Military Service Records: **A Select Catalog of National Archives Microfilm Publications** (1985) is also a helpful resource.

If the compiled military service records have not been reproduced on microfilm, researchers may request to see the original records at the National Archives Building in Washington, DC. Researchers unable to come to Washington may request copies of these records by using NATF Form 86, "National Archives Order for Copies of Military Service Records."

For medical information about soldiers who fought in the Mexican and Civil Wars, consult carded medical records found in Record Group (RG) 94, Records of the Adjutant General's Office, 1780's–1917, entry 534. These cards relate to volunteers admitted to hospitals for treatment and may include information such as name, rank, organization, complaint, date of admission, hospital to which admitted, and date returned to duty, deserted, discharged, sent to general hospital, furloughed, or died.

This series is arranged by state, there under by the number of the regiment (cavalry, infantry, and artillery are filed together under the common regiment number) and then by initial letter of surname. For example, the First Pennsylvania Cavalry is filed under "1 Pennsylvania" along with the First Pennsylvania Infantry, First Pennsylvania Heavy Artillery, First Pennsylvania Light Artillery, and First Pennsylvania Reserves.

Carded medical records of volunteers who served in the Spanish-American War and Philippine Insurrection are filed with the individual's compiled military service record.

Military Records Indexes

Many of these indexes can be found at larger public libraries or at the Family History Center in Salt Lake City. There are many published indexes and compiled records from state and colonial records such as:

Index to Volunteer Soldiers, 1784-1811. Virgil D. White, transcriber, Waynesboro, TN: National Historical Publishing Co., 1987.

Index to Volunteer Soldiers in Indian Wars and Disturbances, 1815-1858. Virgil D. White, transcriber, 2 vols. Waynesboro, TN: National Historical Publishing Co., 1994.

Virginia's Colonial Soldiers. Lloyd Bockstruck, ed., Baltimore, MD: Genealogical Publishing Co., 1988. Reprinted 1998.

Muster Rolls of New York Provincial Troops, 1755-1764, Edward F. DeLancey, ed, 1892. Reprint, Bowie, MD: Heritage Books, 1990.

Colonial Soldiers of the South, 1732-1774. Murtie June Clark, Baltimore, MD: Genealogical Publishing Co., 1983. Reprinted 1999.

Pension Records

Pensions were granted by Congress to invalid or disabled veterans or to their widows if the soldier died in service or because of their service. Generally, there were minimum service or age requirements to receive the benefits. Pensions granted because of disability or injuries sustained in service were called disability or invalid pensions. Service pensions were granted to soldiers meeting minimum service requirements. Widow's pensions were granted to women whose husbands had been killed in the war or were veterans who had served for specified periods of time.

Some states granted early pension benefits to soldiers who served during the Revolutionary War, but the federal government assumed those payments beginning in 1789. The first federal disability pensions were issued in 1792. Most of these records were destroyed by fire in 1800 and 1814.

The first service pensions were granted in 1818 and continued through 1832. In 1780, the Continental Congress provided half-pay pensions to widows and orphans of some officers. This soon expired and not until 1836 did a new act allow widows to apply for pension benefits. Additional acts through 1878 granted more liberal provisions to widows.

Locating Your Ancestor's Name

Many indexes and compilations have been created to help you locate your veteran ancestor including:

Genealogical Abstracts of Revolutionary War Pension Files, Virgil D. White, abstracter. Waynesboro, TN., National Historical Publishing Co., 1990.

Index of Revolutionary War Pension Applications in the National Archives, Washington, D.C.: National Genealogical Society, 1976.

Virginia Revolutionary Pension Applications, John Dorman, 50 vols, Fredericksburg, VA.; the author, 1958-1996.

Additionally, federal census records contain information about military service. The 1840 census asked for names of those receiving pension benefits for Revolutionary service or service after the war. The special census of 1890 provides information on Union Civil War veterans and widows for a limited group of states and the District of Columbia.

The 1910 and 1930 census each ask about military or naval service.

Accessing the Records

If you determine your ancestor may have a pension file at the National Archives, you can request a copy of the file using National Archives Trust Form (NATF) 85. You will need to know at least the following information to request a search:

- Veteran's Name
- State from Which Served
- Branch of Service (Army, Navy, Marine Corps)
- War in Which, or Dates Between Which He Served
- The fees to search and copy records are as follows:
- Full Pension Application File - $80+ (2017)
- Pension Documents Packet - $30 (2017)
- If no file is found, you will not be charged a fee.

You can provide a credit card number to expedite processing of your request.

Information Found in Pension Files

If you request the Pension Documents Packet, you will receive the following eight documents, if present in the file:

- Declaration of pension
- Declaration of widow's pension
- Adjutant General statements of service
- Questionnaires completed by applicants
- Pension dropped cards
- Marriage certificates
- Death certificates
- Discharge certificate

Should you request the full file? In some cases, the full file will contain information that will help in your genealogical research for the veteran and his family. Affidavits from neighbors, friends or relatives of the veteran may be provided to help establish either that the veteran was in the military, that he died from military related service or that the widow-applicant was married to the veteran. You may even find names, dates of birth, places of birth of children and subsequent marriage partners of the widow. If you want a complete picture of the veteran and you don't mind spending a little more money, it may save you hours of research time.

Confederate Pension Records

The National Archives does not maintain records of Confederate pensions. These records are held by the individual states from which the veteran served. You can write to the appropriate state archive for information about your veteran. Again, it is helpful to have as much information about the veteran as possible, such as rank, unit, dates served and branch of service, date of birth, spouse's name and where he lived after the war. Visit http://www.archives.gov/ for more information.

Bounty Land Records

Free land was promised to soldiers to entice them to enter service during the Revolutionary War. State governments began offering land in special military districts soon after the war. The Federal government began providing bounty land warrants after 1800.

Bounty land warrant application files relate to claims based on wartime service between 1775 and March 3, 1855. If your ancestor served in the Revolutionary War, War of 1812, early Indian Wars, or the Mexican War, a search of these records may be worthwhile. Documents found in these records are like those in pension files. Please note that many of the bounty land application files relating to Revolutionary War and War of 1812 service have been combined with the pension files. There is also a series of un-indexed bounty land warrant applications based on service between 1812 and 1855, which includes disapproved applications based on Revolutionary War service.

The act of 1855 provided a bounty of 160 acres to anyone who fought in a battle or served at least fourteen days. It applied to all men who had served in any war up to that time. After 1830, unused warrants could be exchanged for script certificates which would allow the land to be taken up anywhere in the public domain.

These surrendered warrants provide the warrantee's name, names of any heirs filing the claim and their relationship to the warrantees, their places of residence, and the date the warrant was surrendered. These records are indexed and available for researchers.

Using the Records

The National Archives maintain federal bounty land warrant applications for service before 1856. The information provided is like that provided in pension files. It is recommended that pension records be sought first. If no file is found, then apply for the bounty land records.

NATF Form 85 is used to request a search of bounty land files in Washington, D.C. As with pension files, the following information is required:
- Veteran's name
- Branch of service (Army, Navy, Marine Corps)
- State from which he served
- War in which or dates between which, he served

The fee for copying a located file is $30 (2017) This can be paid by credit card to provide for immediate shipping.

Additional Resources:
Index of Revolutionary War Pension Applications in the National Archives, Washington, D.C.: National Genealogical Society, 1976.
Revolutionary War Bounty Land Grants Awarded by State Governments, Lloyd DeWitt Bockstruck, 1996. Reprint, Baltimore, MD: Genealogical Publishing Co., 1998.

Chapter Action Plan
- Determine if the National Archives hold records that relate to your ancestors' military service
- Make a list of each record, where held and where indexes can be searched, if available
- Check any existing indexes for your ancestors file
- Copy down all information found in the index
- Determine where to obtain a copy of the original file, document or resource
- Complete the application or check on-line for the appropriated archive or database
- Keep a record of all documents requested and search results
- Abstract files and keep a copy in your family folder
- Document all sources and maintain proper citation methods

Chapter 12
Federal and State Land Records

I don't know who my grandfather was, I am much more concerned to know what his grandson will be.
--Abraham Lincoln

Land records represent some of the most complete sources of information on early Americans available. From the beginning of the colonial system, land records were maintained to confirm ownership and inheritance from one family to the next. There have been fewer major losses of land and property records over the years than any other type of record. Federal records of public land sales are almost 100% complete. The need to determine ownership interest and resolve disputes required complete records at county court houses. If these records became damaged or lost, a serious effort was made to reconstruct and re-record them.

As immigrants arrived in the U.S. and traveled westward, deeds recorded their movement and documented many aspects of their lives. In many cases, spouses' names appear on land records, as well as children when land is conveyed by will or gift.

We will explore in detail the types of land records available, what can be gleaned from them and where they can be found.

State Land States

As colonies were formed from grants by foreign governments, such as England and Mexico, a process was begun to distribute land to colonists and entrepreneurs. The original colonies, then the states controlled the distribution of land to the first buyer. Subsequent transactions were individual or private land sales.

The state land states include: Connecticut, Delaware, Georgia, Hawaii, Kentucky, Maine, Maryland, Massachusetts, New Hampshire, New Jersey, New York, North Carolina, Pennsylvania, Rhode Island, South Carolina, Tennessee, Texas, Vermont, Virginia and West Virginia.

After the Revolutionary War, all the states ceded lands outside their present-day boundaries to the U.S. government. A portion of this land was used for bounty land warrants. (See the previous chapter)

Survey System of State Land States

Metes and bounds or measurements and markers were primarily used in these early states to survey land. The method was subject to much interpretation and inaccuracy. The process involves selecting a starting point and using compass directions and distance to determine an area of land. Many times, physical landmarks such as trees, rocks and rivers were used to mark the boundaries of the property. Unfortunately, over time these landmarks may change or disappear completely. If you find an old deed of your ancestor with this method of survey, it may be impossible to find the exact location of the property today. States varied in their methods, some employing several different methods even in the same territory.

Additionally, there were Independent Cites, such as Williamsburg, Virginia, that controlled the land process within their borders. Thus, you may need to search city records, not just state or county records to find your ancestor's deed.

State Land Patents

The process of land distribution by a governmental body is called a grant. The original title to the land was in the form of a patent. The patentee would apply at the land office, which may include the county recorder's office, town hall or similar agency. The application included a description of the property, proof of vacancy, any improvements, the estimated value and other information.

If the application was successful, a warrant for survey was issued to mark, plat and record a formal description of the land. The survey was then recorded in the appropriate land office with a description of the property, markers used, natural features and information about adjoining property and their owners. Once the survey was completed and filed, a patent was prepared to transfer official title to the land. This was the first sale of the land. All future sales were recorded as individual or private land transfers.

Most states have indexed their patents and other documents, such as surveys and warrants. Most patents are also recorded in the deed books of the local county or town. Here the grantor is listed as the State.

Accessing the Records

The indexes and records can be found at the state archives or state land office in the state you are researching. Many indexes have been published and can be found in local libraries. Additionally, microfilmed copies of some records are available through local libraries or the Family History Library in Salt Lake City.

On-line Resources

Many States have on-line indexes to their land records. Additionally, other resources can be found with land records databases. Here is a brief sample of some of the sites available on the web:

Arkansas Land Records, *http://searches.rootsweb.com/cgi-bin/arkland/arkland.pl*

Georgia Land Records, *https://familysearch.org/wiki/en/Georgia_Land_and_Property*

Maryland Land Records, *http://guide.mdsa.net/pages/viewer.aspx?page=landrecords*

General land records and related information, Ancestry.com, *http://www.ancestry.com*

Federal Land States

The remaining 30 states that did not fall under the State Land distribution system were controlled by the Federal Land distribution system. As early as 1785, public lands were dispersed by the government to help raise revenue depleted by the Revolutionary War, to compensate soldiers and to expand the frontier through western migration. Land offices were opened as districts were formed to handle land sales in each new area. Over time, as land was dispersed, these districts were merged together until only two Federal land offices remained, the Eastern States office and Western States office.

Survey System of Federal Land States

Unlike the imprecise system of metes and bounds used in colonial states, federal lands were surveyed under the meridian system. A meridian is an imaginary line running directly north and south from pole to pole. Measurements east and west from this line were made at 24-mile increments called guide meridians. To complete the grid, a horizontal line, called a base line is drawn at a right angle to the meridian. From here, north and south increments are made. There are 55 meridians found in the U.S. From these grid coordinates, any parcel of land can be easily located.

Townships are six-mile-squares within the meridian. Ranges are imaginary lines running north and south, set six miles apart. Township directions are the number of blocks, north or south of the base line and range directions are always the number of blocks, east or west of the meridian line. As an example, T1N R3E, would be one township to the north of the base line and three ranges east of the meridian.

Sections are one-mile-square pieces of land that are generally 640 acres in size. There are 36 sections in a township. It is important to note that section numbers start in the northeast corner of a township and move to the left then down and then to the right. Thus, section 1 and section 12 are adjoining. This is important when locating neighbors living close to your ancestor (See figure 12-1)

6	5	4	3	2	1
7	8	9	10	11	12
18	17	16	15	14	13
19	20	21	22	23	24
30	29	28	27	26	25
31	32	33	34	35	36

Figure 12-1, Sectional grid numbering

Sections can be further subdivided into many smaller pieces, such as one-half, one-quarter, one-eighth or even one-thirty second section. (See figure 12-2

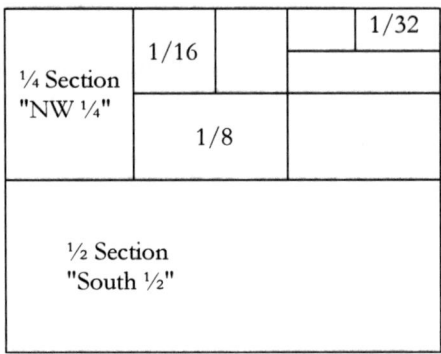

Figure 12-2, Sectional breakdown

Patent Process

As with State-land states, Federal lands required an extensive application process to allow an individual to receive title to the land. As new areas of land were opened, auctions were held and the property went to the highest bidder. The newly opened land office would then offer the remaining land to all comers on a first come, first serve basis. Applicants were required to be either native born or have declared an intention to become a citizen of the United States. A potential landowner would complete an application and submit payment or arrange for credit and be given a receipt. Next, a warrant for survey would be issued to create the survey. The completed survey was recorded in the local township plat books. The registrar would record the information in a tract book.

Land-entry Case Files

The General Land office created files with all the information received for an application. This information can be very valuable for genealogical research. Some of the information might include:

- Declarations of intent
- Affidavits
- Testimonies
- Receipt copies
- Bounty-land warrants
- Proof of citizenship or naturalization
- Rejected, revoked or cancelled claim information

Once approved, the General Land Office would issue a final certificate for the patent. This certificate was proof that the patent was approved and that all steps had been completed properly. The certificate was redeemable for the patent at the local land office. The patent holder was encouraged to register the certificate at the local courthouse for legal protection.

Tract Books

These books hold the history of claims on each piece of property in the federal land system. They are grouped by land office and legal description of township, range and section. Names of each potential purchaser are included, whether rejected, relinquished or finalized. Additional information may include the price per acre and total purchase price, payments made, date of entry and final certificate number. Tract books exist for all federal lands except Missouri and Alaska. They are housed in two locations, the Eastern States Office of the Bureau of Land Management and the National Archives in Washington, DC. The states held by the Eastern office include Alabama, Arkansas, Florida, Illinois, Indiana, Iowa, Louisiana, Michigan, Minnesota, Mississippi, Ohio and Wisconsin. All other Federal land states records are in the National Archives.

Using the Records

All the tract books have been microfilmed and are available through the National Archives, the Family History Library and branch libraries. They may also be found in State Archives, and local and university libraries. To use these records, you must find the tract book that contains the county where your ancestor lived. For example, if your ancestor lived in Colbert County, Georgia, the township range includes 2S to 5S and 9W to 15W from the Huntsville meridian. Tract guides and maps exist for all states and counties to help you locate the tract book.

On-line Research

The Eastern States Office, Bureau of Land Management (BLMBESO), 7450 Boston Boulevard, Springfield VA 22153, has retained custody of the General Land Office tract books for the 13 eastern public land states. BLMBESO also has a computerized index of patented land entries in Alabama, Arkansas, Florida, Illinois, Indiana, Iowa, Louisiana, Michigan, Minnesota, Mississippi, Missouri, Ohio, and Wisconsin. Patents issued by Western states before 1908 are in the BLM state office that has jurisdiction over that territory. See the following site for more information: *http://www.glorecords.blm.gov/visitors/StateResearch.asp*

Portions of this index, called the General Land Office Automated Records System (GLOARS), are available for a fee from the Bureau of Land Management via the Internet. Complete entries from this index give the information needed to locate the case file at NARA. Land offices and types of land entries are given for some states in the system as code numbers, and the final certificate number is called the accession number. GLOARS can be found at the BLM website at: *http://www.glorecords.blm.gov/*

GLOARS provides live access to Federal land conveyance records for the Public Land States. They also provide image access to more than two million Federal land title records for Eastern Public Land States, issued between 1820 and 1908. Images of Serial patents (land titles issued between 1908 and the mid-1960's) are currently being added to this web site. Due to organization of documents in the GLO collection, this site does not currently contain every Federal title record issued for the Public Land States.

GLOARS offers a great way to determine if your ancestor patented land in each state. It can lead to further information and help you pinpoint a location for census, marriage and other research. It also allows you to cover a large geographic area in a short period. The search options let you perform a broad-based search, then narrow down your focus to a specific area, finding not only your ancestor's land, but that of his neighbors, who may be related by blood or marriage. You can also view that actual patent on-line in several formats, such as Gif, Tiff and PDF, plus print or save a copy. If you would like a certified copy, ordering is available on-line as well.

My ancestor, George Hunter lived in Ohio in the early 1800's. I wish to see if he patented land there. A basic search turns up several George Hunters in Ohio. I know from other research, he lived in Knox County. I find a listing for a George Hunter in Knox County and click on the link. It takes me to a page with several tabs. I can view the patent description, legal land description, document image and ordering information for a certified copy. The information I find there can help me locate the tract book that may contain even more information.

The land George Hunter patented was Sec. 19, Twp 7N, Range 10W of Knox County, Ohio in 1835. Looking at my sectional numbering grid (see figure 12-1), I know that section 18 is north, section 20 is east and section 30 is south of section 19. Also, section 24 of Twp, 7n, Rage 11W is west of section 19. If I search all these sections, including section 19 using the standard search engine, I will find all the neighbors of my George Hunter in a two-mile radius of his property. Many times, close neighbors will move together to new lands, intermarry, act as guardians for children and executors or administrators for estates. As I fill in the pieces of the puzzle, this information will become very valuable when I see similar names.

A quick search of section 19, lists another Hunter, John. He may turn out to be a brother, son or other relative. Also in the same section is James Winterringer. I know from county marriage records, a daughter of George married a Winterringer. This may be the father or brother of George's son-in-law. A search of Section 20 finds a Thomas Winterringer, another possible in-law of George. With these names, I can conduct additional research of marriage, probate, census and other records to determine what, if any, connection they have to my ancestor. If my ancestor had a common name, such as Smith or Brown, I can use this information to eliminate unrelated individuals from my research sphere.

Additional Information
   Research in the Land Entry Files of the General Land Office, Record Group 49 , Kenneth Hawkins, compiler, National Archives and Records Administration, 2009,
   https://www.archives.gov/files/publications/ref-info-papers/rip114.pdf

Land & Property Research in the United States, by E. Wade Hone. Salt Lake City: Ancestry, Inc., 1997. *http://www.amazon.com*

Townships and Legal Descriptions of Land, by Charles B. Barr, Independence, MO: the author, 1989.

Ohio Lands and Their Subdivisions, by William E. Peters, Athens, Ohio: the author, 1930.

Chapter Action Plan

- Determine when and where your ancestor may have left land records
- Find the appropriate archive to check land records indexes
- Keep records of all resources checked and results found
- Request copies of records, plats or other documents
- Abstract land transaction details and add them to your family file
- Cite all sources and record location of documents

Chapter 13
Church Records

Genealogy...where you confuse the dead and irritate the living
--Anonymous

The United States was founded by many religious groups seeking freedom from the persecution they experienced in Europe and other parts of the world. Some of the first colonies, such as Pennsylvania, were formed as a haven for religious freedom. Many denominations required records be created of their members' baptism, marriage, burial and attendance. Many of these records survive today and are available for research. Many religious organizations such as the Quakers, kept very detailed records, while others kept very little documentation.

The key to using church records is to determine which church your ancestor may have attended, if records exist and where those records are located. Unfortunately, there is no central repository for church records, such as the National Archives. Many records are kept at the local level or in regional archives. It is important to determine which denomination and which local church your ancestor attended. This may be found in obituaries, biographies, autobiographies, family bibles, family letters, diaries, certificates of baptism, christenings, etc.

Church records vary from denomination and period. Unfortunately, many records were kept by traveling clergy and were lost over time. The following table is a brief outline of major denominations in the U.S. and their record collections.

Church Records Survey

Denomination (Current Name)	Types of Records	Where Records Are Located	Additional Information
Congregational Church (United Church of Christ)	Baptisms, burials, lists of communicants, dismissions and meeting minutes. Ministers did not perform marriages until the latter part of the 17th century.	Local church or Connecticut State Library, New Hampshire Historical Society, R.H. Cook Collection, Congregational Library	http://www.ucc.org/ http://www.cslib.org/ http://www.nhhistory.org/
Church of England (Protestant Episcopal Church)	Baptisms, marriages and burials.	Local parish or dioceses.	http://www.episcopalarchives.org/ http://www.uri.edu/library/ http://www.newyorkfamilyhistory.org/

54

Denomination	Records	Repository	Website
Presbyterian Church	Records of the session and trustees may contain baptisms, deaths and membership transfers	Presbyterian Historical Society, Historical Foundation of the Presbyterian and Reformed Churches	http://www.history.pcusa.org/
Lutheran and German Reformed Churches	Baptisms and list of communicants, some marriage and burial records. Many records are in German.	Lutheran Archives Center, Abdel Ross Wentz Library, Archives of the American Lutheran Church, Evangelical and Reformed Historical Society	http://www.lacphila.org/ https://www.elca.org https://erhs.info/
Society of Friends (Quakers)	Births, deaths, marriage certificates, minutes of monthly meetings	Encyclopedia of American Quaker Genealogy, Friends Historical Library	http://www.ancestry.com http://www.swarthmore.edu/Library/friends/ http://library.haverford.edu/places/special-collections/
Roman Catholic Church	Registers of baptisms, confirmations, marriages and deaths.	Local parish. See the Official Catholic Directory for addresses.	http://www.officialcatholicdirectory.com/OCD/home
Methodist Church	Records of baptisms, marriages and membership after 1800. Some death records after 1900. Some personal journals of circuit riding ministers exist.	Local church, United Methodist Archives Center	http://gcah.org/ https://www.bu.edu/sthlibrary/
Baptist Church	Few records of genealogical interest. Mostly membership records	Local church, American Baptist Convention, American Baptist Historical Society	http://abhsarchives.org/
Jewish Synagogues	Birth and circumcision records, bar/bat mitzvah and confirmation records, some marriage, death and burial records.	Local synagogue, American Jewish Archives, American Jewish Historical Society.	http://www.americanjewisharchives.org/aja/index.html http://www.ajhs.org/ http://www.cjh.org/pdfs/Landsmanschaftn.pdf

Microfilmed Collections
　　The Family History Library in Salt Lake City has microfilmed many church records from around the world. Once you have determined your ancestor's local church membership, you should contact that church and ask about records they hold. If they are not willing to search the records for you, or you are not able to travel to that location, check the Family History Library on-line catalog to see if they may hold the records. If you cannot visit the main library in Salt Lake City, you can request the needed microfilm be sent to a local branch library near you.

Additional On-line Resources
　　http://www.awesomegenealogy.com/churchrecords.shtml
　　https://familysearch.org/wiki/en/United_States_Church_Records
　　http://www.bac-lac.gc.ca/eng/discover/vital-statistics-births-marriages-deaths/Pages/church-records-indexes.aspx

Published Resources
　　The Researcher's Guide to American Genealogy, by Val D. Greenwood, Baltimore: Genealogical Publishing Co., 3rd ed, 2002.
　　Encyclopedia of American Quaker Genealogy, by William Hinshaw, Baltimore: Genealogical Publishing Co., 1936-1950, reprint ed.

Chapter Action Plan
- Make a list of the local church membership and denomination for each ancestor gathered from obituaries, biographies, confirmation or baptism certificates or other information
- Contact the local church office to see what records, if any are held there for the period you seek
- Determine if there is a regional archive for the records you need
- Properly document and cite each source used to prove information in your database

Chapter 14
Genealogical Software

Theory of relativity: If you go back far enough, we're all related
--Anonymous

Now that you have begun to accumulate data, photographs and other family history materials, you will want to organize your data, produce reports and share your information with others.

As personal computers have evolved over the years, so has family history software. Today's programs are very sophisticated and can provide you with many useful tools and features. Additionally, the price has dropped from hundreds of dollars for a DOS-based program to less than $50 for a full-featured Windows or Mac-based program.

Before you purchase a software program, you need to think about what you expect the software to provide and how you are going to use it. Also, what platform to use, Windows or Mac and whether you plan to use your phone or tablet to record or retrieve information.

Features

Today's software offers many features to enhance your family research experience. Some allow you to add photographs, voice clips, music and even video clips to your project. Others allow you to create web pages to display your family history research and share your progress with fellow researchers.

I enjoy creating charts, both family group and pedigree to help me "visualize" my family history progress. It is important to me to have very flexible chart functions and crisp, easy to read output. I use these charts in my research to quickly determine what I have and what I still need. If you desire this type of organization and reporting, you will want a program with great charts.

With the growing use of portable electronics, many family history researchers want to take their databases to the library to check information or add notes and view portions of your database for research purposes.

Try it before you buy it

Most programs today allow you to download a trial version that allows you to try it out, before spending your hard-earned cash. You then either become a registered user of the base program (usually for free), or you upgrade to the deluxe version for a fee. Try several different programs before you settle on one. Some researchers maintain more than one software system to allow them to use features found only in certain programs, while keeping the maximum possible flexibility. As an example, perhaps you will be working closely with a distant relative who has been using Software "X" for many years. To allow the best possible transfer of information back and forth, you decide to also use this same system on your computer. The two of you can now send files back and forth with minimum loss of data. You may decide to also maintain another program "Y" because it provides you with features not found in "X".

As you test out a new program, add a few families to determine the ease of imputing data and building family relationships. Does it automatically ask about a marriage date when you create a mother and father relationship? Can you add siblings easily without having to re-connect the children to each parent? How easy is it to locate a specific individual in your database using a name list? One common issue is multiple individuals with the same name. How can you quickly sort them out? If you have duplicate entries of the same person, how do you correct that problem? These are just a few of the tests you will want to complete before selecting your primary database program.

GEDCOM

As discussed in Chapter 7, GEDCOM allows you to share genealogical data with other researchers using different software programs. The problem is in the translation. Some programs are better than others at importing data with minimal loss. Source citations are critical elements that cannot be lost when a GEDCOM file is added to your database. As part of your initial testing, you will want to create GEDCOM files and import them into different programs to see how the data is handled. Many programs create an error report showing what was not transferred so you can go back and make corrections as needed.

Writing your book

If your ultimate goal is to publish your work, you will want a program that makes this task as easy as possible. Some programs will produce camera ready copy for your publication, or export your information into another prepress program. Depending on your level of technological sophistication, you could provide the publisher an electronic file that will be used to print the book. Before investing heavily in software with a long learning curve, you will want to talk to several publishers and decide the best method for your future book. (See Chapter 21 for more details)

Software Programs

Below find a list of some of the most popular software programs on the market today. It is not an exhaustive list by any means. Contact the manufacturer for more details and free trial offers.

Windows Based Software

Program Name	Software Publisher	Website
Ancestral Quest	Incline Software, LC	http://www.ancquest.com
DoroTree (Jewish Genealogy)	Manachat Technology Park	http://www.dorotree.com
Family Tree Maker	Genealogy.com	http://www.genealogy.com/soft_ftm.html
Legacy	Millennia Corporation	http://www.legacyfamilytree.com
Personal Ancestral File	The Church of Jesus Christ of Latter-Day Saints	http://www.familysearch.org
RootsMagic	FormalSoft, Inc.	http://www.rootsmagic.com
The Master Genealogist	Wholly Genes Software	http://www.whollygenes.com

Macintosh Based Software

Program Name	Software Publisher	Website
Heredis	BSD Concept	http://www.myheredis.com
Reunion	Leister Productions	http://www.leisterpro.com

Chapter Action Plan

- If you are ready for a genealogy software program, determine your needs and goals
- Check out several programs before selecting one as your primary database
- Pick one that will meet your needs and grow with your research
- Add your family information, being careful to add source citations

Chapter 15
Free On-Line Databases

I'd rather look for dead people than have 'em look for me!
--Anonymous

One of the most important milestones in the history of genealogical research is the creation of the Internet, the resulting access to large amounts of data and the ability to easily contact other researchers.

In the not too distant past, two different family history researchers could be compiling a book on the same family and not know about each other. Even though this could still happen today, it is less likely, because of the resources available on the web.

We will examine the types of information that can be found on large genealogical databases, plus how researchers can not only find family information, but find each other.

Technology and Innovation

As soon as the initial stages of the Internet were being accessed by "early adopters", the potential for genealogical research quickly became apparent. Here was a tool that allowed huge databases from around the world to be quickly researched. It has been predicted that at some time in the future, nearly everyone's family tree will have been compiled by someone and stored on the web, just waiting for you to add the missing link. That goal may someday be reached as millions of pages of materials are being added daily.

As an example, the SSDI, or Social Security Death Index contains a list of over 72 million names of persons with Social Security numbers whose deaths have been reported to the Social Security Administration. The death may have been reported by a survivor requesting benefits. The system was computerized in 1962 and over 90% of the reported deaths occurred after 1962. In the past you would need to request this information in writing from the Social Security Administration. With today's technology, you can search the entire database for free. *http://search.ancestry.com/search/db.aspx?dbid=3693*

The information on file includes the name of the deceased, social security number, date of birth, date of death, last place of residence and the state of residence at the time the social security card was issued. With this information, you can search for a death record, census information, an obituary and request a copy of the social security application. Many other databases are being digitized and made available for research. We will review some of the most comprehensive collections and what they offer.

Web-based Genealogical Databases
RootsWeb.com, *http://www.rootsweb.com*

This large collection is run by volunteers to provide a wide variety of services to the genealogical community. Foremost is the Surname List, a registry of more than 1 million surname entries that have been submitted by more than 250,000 individuals. General information, such as dates and locations are listed with information on how to contact the submitter to exchange more details. This allows you to find fellow researchers who may have information you seek.

You can also join a surname mailing list, which is a list of submissions distributed to everyone on the list by email. You can see what others are discussing about a common surname and submit your own query to receive feedback from fellow researchers. You might even discover a long-lost cousin. There are over 28,000 such lists covering surnames, U.S. counties and states, other countries and regions, ethnic groups and related topics.

Message boards offer a computerized version of the bulletin board. You can search through over 130,000 message boards relating to surnames, localities and related topics. Your posting will help others find you as you continue your research.

Another method of finding existing research is with the **World Connect Project**, a database of family trees submitted by researchers and indexed on the website. Currently, over 328 million names are found through multiple search engines. Once you find a likely ancestor, you can view a family and pedigree chart (if submitted), plus download a multi-generation GEDCOM file, if provided by the submitter.

As with other GEDCOM files, care should be taken to confirm all names, dates and places with your own primary source research. Many of these files have been passed around the Internet with no verification of the facts. This can give you a false since of security that the data is correct because you have seen it so many times and on so many databases. This represents one of the may hazards of "instant" family trees.

FamilySearch.org, *http://www.familysearch.org*

The Family History Library of The Church of Jesus Christ of Latter-day Saints has one of the largest collections of genealogical records in the world. Over 2.2 million rolls of microfilm, 742,000 microfiche, 300,000 books and 4,500 periodicals are just part of the collection. In the past you had to travel to Salt Lake City, or visit a local branch library to view a catalog of materials. With the Internet, you can now view this catalog instantly. Once you have made your list, you can request those items through the branch library loan program or visit the main library in person. The catalog is updated constantly with new materials.

Church members have been submitting pedigree charts and family group sheets to the Ancestral File database for over 50 years. Now this collection of over 35 million names can be researched on the Internet. Once matches have been found, you can contact the submitter for more information.

The International Genealogical Index is a collection of events, such as birth, christening, marriage, death and burial. This information comes from original records microfilmed by the church and submissions by individuals. The collection today includes over 600 million names with an additional 135 million found in an addendum. The records include both US and many foreign countries. The microfilm process continues in recently opened locations, such as Russia, Romania and other former communist countries. Records from over 110 countries, territories and possessions can be found in the Index and library holdings.

The USGenWeb Project, *http://www.usgenweb.com*

Run by volunteers, this project consists of links to resources available on every county in the U.S. The county coordinator provides both submitted and original materials, such as tax lists, census records, newspaper files and related materials. On a larger scale, state and national projects target larger databases, such as census, tombstone and marriages to allow someone with little family history information to pinpoint a location to target their research. Before visiting a county courthouse in person, you are encouraged to access the county GenWeb site and gather as much information as possible to allow maximum use of your research time when at the courthouse.

Wikipedia: *https://www.wikipedia.org/*

Wikipedia is written by volunteers and contains a wealth of information such as locations, historical figures, battles, local history, photographs, maps and much more. You can use this to locate a castle or church that your ancestor may have visited or the location of a battle they fought in.

Chapter Action Plan

- Research web-based database sites to determine what information about your ancestors may be available
- Use potential links to further your research, pinpoint research locations and gather sources
- Verify and document all information before using the data to prove a family relationship, date or location
- Join surname and county email lists to find fellow researchers and determine what research exists on your family lines

Chapter 16
A Picnic at the Cemetery

*Show me the first graveyards of a county and I will tell
you the true character of the people.*
--Benjamin Franklin

As some point in your research, you will want to see great-grandfather Zachariah's final resting place. You might also be able to get additional information needed for your research, such as date of birth, date of death, spouses and children's names, etc. The tombstone might be the only place you can find this information. Unfortunately, with the march of time, pollution, vandalism, urban sprawl, flooding and neglect, the tombstone and even the cemetery itself, may no longer exist. The first task is to locate the potential site of Zachariah's burial.

Cemetery Types and Locations
Cemeteries in the U.S. can be categorized as four primary types:
Family cemetery.
Usually found in rural communities or sparsely populated areas. A small piece of the family farm or ranch was set aside to bury family members. Over time the land was sold and the cemetery location forgotten. The new land owner may not even know that a cemetery once existed and has since used the land for other purposes. Even if the cemetery still exists, you might not be able to get permission from the current landowner to access the property.

To find this type of cemetery, you must research other records, such as obituaries, biographies, family bibles, deed records, letters and compiled cemetery records. These can be found at the local library, courthouse or historical society. Once you have found a cemetery located on private property, you should visit the county clerk's office to determine the current owner and obtain the owner's phone number.

Explain that you are researching your family history and believe an ancestor is buried on their property. They may confirm this or tell you that no cemetery or headstones still exist. If they do agree to allow you to visit the site, schedule a convenient time when they can meet you on the property and show you where the cemetery is located. Do not drive or walk the property alone. You might get lost or trespass where the owner doesn't want you. Bring your camera (see photo techniques later in this chapter) and take lots of photos. You might not find an existing tombstone, but you can get a since of the location and add to your family file.

Community Cemeteries. Some of the most common types of cemeteries are those created with donated property from local land owners, or created from land purchased by the local community government. These cemeteries are normally well maintained and are easily accessible. Here you might be able to find several generations of ancestors buried together with children, grandchildren along with their spouses. In farming communities, families intermarried, worshiped at the same church and were buried in the same cemetery. Records can be found at the city clerk's office, local library or local historical society.

Privately Owned Cemeteries. More common in modern times, these corporate-owned cemeteries are found in most large cities. They are very well maintained and keep excellent records. Many of these records have been published and are available at the local library. Others can be accessed by calling the cemetery office directly or visiting in person. Many maintain detailed plot maps that can assist you in finding the right burial location. Because of perpetual maintenance and excellent security, the chance of vandalism and tombstone damage is much less than at other cemeteries.

Church Owned Cemeteries. In the New England states, burials were made right in the churchyard. Here you can find tombstones dating from the 1600's. As the churchyard became crowded, the church found other plots of land to bury their dead. These cemeteries may or may not be well maintained depending on the resources available to the church. The church may have closed, moved or sold the cemetery to another organization. The church (if still in existence) should have burial records. You may also be able to find them at the local library or city clerk's office. In larger, well-maintained cemeteries, a sexton's office is available and provides records and plot maps. Call ahead before you visit to determine what information is available to aid your research and hours of operation.

GPS Technology

Global Positioning System (GPS) technology is now available for personal use. If you own a GPS receiver, you may be able to use this device to find your ancestor's cemetery. You must have the coordinates of the cemetery before you can input them. One method is to check the United States Geological Survey (USGS) tool called GNIS or Graphical Names Information System, http://geonames.usgs.gov. Here you can enter the name of the cemetery and it will give you GPS coordinates and the topographical (topo) map that covers that area. You might want to review the topo map to make sure you are in the right area. The topo map may contain other local cemeteries that are not found on the GNIS database. Topo maps can be purchased directly from the USGS, local map stores or from Mytopo.com, http://www.mytopo.com. or Topozone.com, http://www.topozone.com/. Once you have your maps and/or GPS coordinates, you are ready to hit the road!

Cemetery Records

Cemetery records can be divided into two groups, tombstone and burial records. Tombstones are the markers found in the cemetery and burial records are created when the deceased was interred. If the cemetery has a sexton's office, there is a good chance that they will have burial records.

Most tombstones will have the name of the deceased, date of death and age at death, expressed as years, months and days. The stone may also contain the name of the spouse, names of children, military service, religious affiliation and parents' names. More recent tombstones may have actual date of birth, place of birth and place of death. The amount of information varies widely with location, time and age of the deceased. If a man dies of advanced age, leaving behind many children and grandchildren and was a pillar in the community, then there is a good chance the tombstone or monument will be larger and more ornate than for a younger man with no children. Children who die young may only have a small stone with their name and date of death.

Burial records may contain no more information than that found on the tombstone, but may tell you the actual date of burial, the person who purchased the plot and the funeral home involved with the burial. This may lead to additional information from the funeral director. If the burial records are indexed or computerized, you may be able to request a list of all individuals buried in the cemetery with the same last name as your ancestor, or the names of related families. This can become valuable later as you expand your research!

Tombstone Photography

Once you locate your ancestor's tombstone, you will want to make a photographic record. Many tombstones are ornate and contain lines of poetry, bible verses or song lyrics. This information helps create a better understanding of the personality and values of your ancestor. To be prepared to take good photographs, you will need the following toolkit:

- Digital camera (high resolution)
- Solid tripod
- Grass clippers
- Small hand trowel or shovel
- Small soft-bristled brush
- Mirror (at least 12" square or larger)
- Mirror stand or tripod
- Work clothes and walking shoes
- Bug repellent (summer)
- Notebook or legal pad of paper
- Work gloves
- Bottle of water
- Road maps, plot maps

As you can see, to be fully prepared will take some space in your car. If you are flying to the cemetery location, you will want to take compact versions of these items, or purchase them when you arrive at your destination.

When you arrive at the cemetery, take pictures of the sign, front gate or archway that provides the name of the cemetery. Once you finish your tombstone photographs, you will take another of the same sign to bookmark your photos. If you visit several cemeteries you will soon lose track of which photos belong to which cemetery. You will also want to keep a log of photos taken, the name, dates of birth and death, and other information you find on the tombstone of the deceased. When you get back home and look at your photos, you may not be able to read the tombstone information. A digital camera makes this much easier, because you can see your results at the site and retake as needed to get a clear shot.

Once you locate your ancestor's tombstone, you may find it broken, covered with weeds, grass or dirt, sunken in the ground, covered with moss or lichen and weathered so much, you cannot read the inscription. You should not attempt to make any major change to the stone, such as trying to reset it, clean it or move it. Leave this to the local caretakers. Report any vandalism or stone damage immediately to the appropriate party. If your ancestor's stone is damaged beyond repair, you might want to consider purchasing a new one and have it professionally set.

Attempting to clean the stone may cause more damage by scratching the soft surface. Never use shaving cream, soap or other cleaning products. Only use a soft bristle brush if needed to remove dirt, leaves or other debris. Use a little clean water if necessary to clean dirt off the stone. Do not attempt to remove the lichen. Use your grass clippers to cut weeds or tall grass by hand to better see the stone and use your hand trowel to gently move dirt that may cover the bottom of the stone. I do not recommend making a rubbing of the stone, as this may damage it further and in many cases, fail to provide you a clear impression of the words and dates.

A far better method involves using your mirror to angle sunlight on to the face of the stone. You may have to experiment with many angles before you get the best reflection. If you have a partner with you, it makes the job much easier, one holding the mirror and the other looking through the camera viewfinder until the right lighting is achieved. Take photos of the entire stone and then close-ups of the dates and wording. If you have time, walk the entire cemetery looking for other family names on your tree. Finish your visit by taking a parting shot of the cemetery sign to remind you later which stones belong to which cemetery. Don't forget to properly document your cemetery sources when adding them to your family database (See Chapter 7 for more information).

Additional Resources:
Tombstone birthday calculator, *http://www.searchforancestors.com/utility/birthday.html*
On-line Databases:
https://www.findagrave.com/
https://billiongraves.com/

Chapter Action Plan
- Make a list of your ancestors buried in each area you plan to visit
- Using cemetery lists, maps and other aids, try to locate the cemetery and determine if it is open to the public
- If on private lands, arrange with the land owner to visit the site
- Take you cemetery kit and be ready for lots of walking and searching
- Once you find the right tombstone, take lots of pictures and use a mirror to highlight the wording
- Document your findings and cite all sources

Chapter 17
Genealogical Societies

I looked for my ancestors...and I found friends
--Anonymous

Once you get started tracking down your roots, it is helpful to share your experiences with others and learn new techniques. Most major metropolitan areas offer one or more genealogical or historical societies. These groups often have monthly or quarterly meetings, special guest lecturers and publish a newsletter. This is a great way to improve your research skills and learn from professionals in the field. National organizations offer comprehensive services, such as annual conferences, monthly newsletters, quarterly periodicals and database services. We will explore both the local and major national groups and what they can provide you to assist in your research efforts.

Local Societies

Genealogical and historical societies exist in almost every county in the country. Larger cities may have several groups. There is a good chance you can find a group near where you live. The goal of most groups is to help their members with genealogical challenges. They do this in a multitude of ways, such as:

- Regular membership meetings with guest speakers
- Periodic newsletters focused on techniques and local history
- Annual or semi-annual workshops with professional lecturers or published authors
- A query column containing requests for information from local or distant members
- An affiliation with the local library's department of genealogy to provide workshops, lock-ins and other training programs

Locate a society near you and attend a meeting or two to determine if you would like to join. Ask other members about the types of programs and services available to members. As you expand your search to distant counties, you may want to join a society located in your ancestor's county or community. This is a great way to get local information, send queries and determine if other members are researching your family line. You may even find a long-lost cousin or two! Some newsletters allow you to submit a query without becoming a member, usually for a small fee.

Family Associations

Family associations may exist just for planning annual family reunions or for more scholarly pursuits, such as preserving family history. Some have very large membership bases, while others a few hundred. Most large metropolitan libraries subscribe to many family association newsletters and you can research the ones relating to your family names to see if it may be worth becoming a member, submitting a query or even visiting a family reunion. Many of these groups have produced published family histories as well.

Finding local societies and family associations

Several sources exist to help you find local, regional or national societies and associations:

- Contact your local library
- Contact the local library in your ancestor's community
- FamilySearch.org,
  https://familysearch.org/wiki/en/United_States_Societies
- Consult **Ulrich's International Periodicals Directory** at your local library
- Consult the **Directory of Family Associations**, by Elizabeth P. Bentley, (Baltimore, MD: The Genealogical Publishing Co., 2001),
  http://www.genealogical.com/item_detail.asp?afid=1132&ID=426
- Search the **Federation of Genealogical Societies** (FGS) website at *http://www.fgs.org/*
- Search the county website at US Gen Web, *http://www.usgenweb.org/*

National & Regional Societies

The New England Historic Genealogical Society (NEHGS), http://www.americanancestors.org/

Formed in 1845, it is the oldest genealogical society in the U.S., with over 20,000 members worldwide. The focus is New England ancestors, to which most Americans can trace some part of their family history. The society publishes two primary periodicals, the bi-monthly New England Ancestors and quarterly, The New England Historical Genealogical Register.

NEHGS offers a diverse array of lectures, public seminars, tours, intensive research programs, and conferences for genealogists of all levels. Programs range from regional conferences to week-long research programs.

NEHGS library

Since 1845 NEHGS has collected a vast number of genealogical materials related to New England and beyond. NEHGS also provides a highly trained research staff, professional librarians, and volunteers who are eager to help you in your research. NEHGS provides an on-line library card catalog. Here you will find more than 200,000 genealogical and historical volumes, countless manuscripts, and other special sources. The R. Stanton Avery Collections feature over two million manuscript items ranging from the seventeenth century to the present covering New England and other regions.

The National Genealogical Society (NGS), *http://www.ngsgenealogy.org*
Founded in 1903 as a non-profit organization, the National Genealogical Society is a large and growing membership of individuals and other groups from all over the country—and the world—that share a common love of the field of genealogy.

The society publishes two primary periodicals, the bi-monthly NGS Newsmagazine and the NGS Quarterly, published since 1912. NGS also publishes many how-to books, research guides and reference books covering all aspects of local and international research methods.

NGS sponsors an annual national conference featuring multiple workshop tracks for both the beginner and more experienced genealogist. Additionally, exhibitors offer convention attendees a wide range of products and services, such as books, software, publishing services and more.

The society offers a home study course for beginning genealogists, called American Genealogy: A Basic Course. The course, which is accredited by the Distance Education and Training Council, is designed for all family historians wanting to research their ancestors more effectively and efficiently. Sixteen lessons introduce each of the major record groups used in American genealogical research and require "hands-on" experience. Students are given instruction in basic record keeping, source documentation, and evaluation of evidence.

The circulating collection of the National Genealogical Society is located at the St. Louis County Library (SLCL) in Missouri. The collection consists of 20,000+ books and new titles are being added daily. Every book in the NGS Special Collection at St. Louis is available for Interlibrary Loan to NGS members and non-members alike.

GENTECH

GENTECH, a division of the National Genealogical Society, facilitates communication among persons interested in genealogy and technology. By presenting national conferences, sponsoring programs with other societies, and publishing white papers based on analyses of problems of common interest to genealogists and technologists, they seek to maximize the movement of knowledge among the members of the organization.

http://www.ngsgenealogy.org/cs/GenTech

New York Genealogical and Biographical Society (NYG&B)
http://www.newyorkfamilyhistory.org/

The New York Genealogical and Biographical Society, popularly known as the "G & B," was founded in 1869. As a non-profit educational institution, it's mission is to collect and make available information on genealogy, biography and history, particularly as it relates to the people of New York state.

The G&B provides its members access to all of the library's collections (books, manuscripts, and microforms); subscriptions to two quarterly publications, the Record and the Newsletter, and discounts on other publications; four free queries per year in the Newsletter (also reprinted on the website);

access to the NYG&B Community Bulletin Board; remote access to the ProQuest® Historical Newspapers New York Times database and HeritageQuest™ through the NYG&B's website; and reduced fees for educational programs and the library's record search service.

G&B Library

The G&B maintains one of the principal genealogical reference libraries in the United States. The collection consists of more than 75,000 books, 1,300 periodicals, some 30,000 manuscripts, and nearly 22,000 microforms, as well as computer media. The Library's major focus is New York State genealogy and local history. For New York's colonial period, the Library's resources are unexcelled, and there are also impressive holdings for 19th and early 20th century New York State research, including all the available federal and state censuses through 1925.

Manuscript Collection

This collection contains more than 30,000 unpublished and unique items, ranging from 16th-century deeds to research notes on 20th-century families. Among the items are transcriptions of New York church and cemetery records, genealogical charts, maps, personal diaries, vital records from family Bibles, and the compiled notes of prominent genealogists and historians, such as Kenn and Harriet Stryker-Rodda, Josephine Frost, Innes Getty, Alfred Vail, and Asa Fitch, among others. Members of the NYG&B have access to the Manuscript Collection in person. Members and non-members have access to it through the Record Search Service.

Lineage Societies

Since Americans cannot hold royal titles, we have sought to connect to the past generations in other ways. Lineage societies began forming in the 1800s to honor military service and to preserve family history. The largest such organization is the Daughters of the American Revolution (DAR), founded in 1890 for female descendants of Revolutionary War patriots.

Daughters of the American Revolution (DAR) , *http://www.dar.org/default.cfm*

As one of the largest genealogical societies in the country, DAR boasts 170,000 members in 3,000 chapters across the United States and internationally. Any woman 18 years or older-regardless of race, religion, or ethnic background, who can prove lineal descent from a patriot of the American Revolution, is eligible for membership.

To become a member, applicants must prove they are descended from a Revolutionary War patriot. In the past, documentation was lax and potentially unreliable to current applicants. Today's standards are much more stringent, requiring certified copies of bible records, census records, probate records, military records and detailed proof for each generation back to the patriot.

DAR Patriot Index

The DAR Patriot Index has been an indispensable genealogical tool for DAR members and prospective members for almost 40 years. The newly revised DAR Patriot Index consists of more than 126,000 names of those Patriots, both men and women, who have been accepted by the DAR genealogical staff as having contributed to the cause of American Independence.

This three-volume set includes such information (when it is known) as the Patriot's:
- date and place of birth and death
- state or country of service
- type of service for which credited
- name of spouse(s)

The release of the new Millennium Edition of the DAR Patriot Index is a noteworthy publication because of how infrequently this set of records has been printed. The Millennium Edition is a revised version of the DAR Patriot Index that was published in 1994 and is only the third edition since its inception in 1966. It includes the names of the ancestors of DAR members and other individuals whose service has been recognized by the DAR.

The Patriot Index is found in most major libraries or can be ordered from the DAR. Also, an on-line look up service is available at: *http://services.dar.org/public/dar_research/search/?Tab_ID=1*

The DAR will provide copies of previous membership applications for a fee. If you know a relative that has been admitted based on their connection to a patriot, you may be able to use their prior research. However, keep in mind that older membership applications did not require the type of documentation and proof now required. You can request a copy of a prior membership application by completing the on-line form: *http://services.dar.org/Public/DAR_Research/record_copy/?action=overview*

DAR Library in Washington, DC

The DAR library houses one of the largest collections of genealogy related materials in the U.S. You will find published genealogies, biographies, manuscripts, compilations, periodicals and other research materials. The library is open to members and non-members alike. A trip to Washington must include this valuable collection. Additionally, the library offers an on-line card catalog.

National Society of the Sons of the American Revolution (SAR, *http://www.sar.org/*

In 1876 there were many celebrations to commemorate the centennial of the signing of the Declaration of Independence on July 4, 1776. As part of this patriotic fervor, a group of men in the San Francisco, California, area who were descendants of patriots involved in the American Revolution, formed an organization called the Sons of Revolutionary Sires. Their objective was to have a fraternal and civic society to salute those men and women who pledged their lives, fortunes and sacred honor to the battle for independence from Great Britain. They desired to keep alive their ancestors' story of patriotism and courage in the belief that it is a universal one of man's struggle against tyranny -- a story which would inspire and sustain succeeding generations when they would have to defend and extend our freedoms.

Out of the Sires grew the National Society of the Sons of the American Revolution, which was organized on April 30, 1889 -- the 100th anniversary of the inauguration of George Washington. The SAR was conceived as a fraternal and civic society composed of lineal descendants of the men who wintered at Valley Forge, signed the Declaration of Independence, fought in the battles of the American Revolution, served in the Continental Congress, or otherwise supported the cause of American Independence.

The National Society was chartered by an Act of the United States Congress on June 6, 1906. The charter was signed by President Theodore Roosevelt, who was a member of the SAR. The charter authorizes the granting of charters to societies of the various states and territories and authorizes the state societies to charter chapters within their borders.

To be eligible for membership, individuals must be a citizen of good repute in the community and the lineal descendant of an ancestor who was always unfailing in loyalty to the cause of American independence and rendered acceptable service by overt acts of resistance to the authority of Great Britain. The patriotic service and line of descent must be documented through acceptable references. Family tradition regarding the service of an ancestor or the line of descent is not acceptable as documentation.

NSSAR Library

The NSSAR Historical and Genealogical Library is a comprehensive reference and research facility, with over 50,000 items (books, microfilms, etc), located in Louisville, KY. Some of the primary materials include,

- The George Washington Collection consists of the Morristown Manuscript Collection and the George Washington Papers: 1,200 books and 750 journal articles
- Family histories - microfiche of 8,000 family histories books, half of which are out of print and no longer available from the publishers
- State genealogical materials, concentrating heavily on New England, New York, Pennsylvania, and Virginia
- Federal census - 8,000 reels of microfilm. For about half of the states they have the entire series from 1790 to 1920. The series for the other states are gradually being completed
- Genealogy search programs produced by the Church of Jesus Christ of Latter Day Saints (also known as the Mormon Church)

- Automated Archives CD Collection - there are many CD-ROMs in this collection, including Family Tree Maker
- Revolutionary War pension applications on microfilm

Chapter Action Plan
- Determine which genealogical societies may offer you support and educational opportunities
- Visit local groups and participate in future workshops
- If you wish to join a lineage society, determine membership requirements and map out a plan to provide proper documentation
- Join regional or state associations that focus on your current family research project. Assess their on-line resources, library holdings, publications and other member benefits

Chapter 18
Immigrant Ancestors

Only a Genealogist regards a step backwards as progress
--Unknown

At some point in your research, you will trace an ancestral line back to the first immigrant to arrive in the U.S. Depending on your family, this could have occurred at any time in the past 400 years. The further back you travel in time, the more difficult the search. If you are lucky to have a connection to a famous historical figure, such as colonial governor, founding father or Mayflower passenger, this research may have already been completed for you. However, for most of us who have descended from common stock, it will mean lots of hard work to find the homeland of our ancestors.

Getting Started

Before you attempt to trace your family line beyond the U.S. border, keep in mind the following:

- Do as much research in the U.S. as possible. Many foreign databases such as census, records are becoming available for U.S. researchers. Use them now to narrow down your research focus
- Unless you speak and read the language of your ancestor's homeland, it will be very difficult to understand what is available and how to find it. You might want to consider hiring a local professional genealogist to research original records for you. (See Chapter 19 for more information)
- Country boundaries and political systems have changed dramatically over the past 400 years. Your ancestor may have come from a part of the world that has shifted political control several times. The records you seek may be held in several different countries and various governmental archives
- The types of records and location of records is considerably different than those found in the U.S
- Research passenger lists and immigration records to determine if your ancestor can be found on a ship's list, when he or she immigrated and from which country they came. (See Chapter 10 for more information)
- If possible, visit the Family History Library in Salt Lake City. They have an extensive collection of foreign records on microfilm and have staff that can read the language in which they were written

The following is a brief list of some of the research aids that are available for countries from which a large portion of the U.S. population today can trace their roots. This information changes daily and should not be considered all inclusive.

England & British Isles

England established the first permanent settlements on the east coast of colonial America beginning in 1608, with Jamestown, Virginia. Soon huge numbers of immigrants sought religious and economic freedoms in the New World.

Vital Records

Births, marriages and deaths in England and Wales since 1 July 1837 can be obtained by visiting the General Register Office, GRO, PO Box 2, Southport Merseyside PR8 2JD. Names, dates, ages, addresses and occupations can be obtained. The National Archives has census records for the years 1851, 1861, 1871, 1881, and 1891. *http://www.nationalarchives.gov.uk/*

Births, marriages and deaths before 1837 can be found in the International Genealogical Index (IGI) on the FamilySearch website at *http://www.familysearch.org/*.

Index of archives, repositories and special collections of parish, town, village and county records, *http://www.nationalarchives.gov.uk/*

Wills before 1858

Before 1858 wills were proved in a variety of church and other courts. The location of a person's personal property, and its overall value, determined which court was appropriate. The two chief courts were the Prerogative Court of Canterbury (PCC, mainly concerned with personal estates of people roughly south of the Midlands, and those dying abroad leaving property in the UK), and the Prerogative Court of York (PCY), with jurisdiction over the northern counties. The records of this court, 1388-1858, are held at Borthwick Institute of Historical Research, St Anthony's Hall, Peasholme Green, York YO1 2PW (Telephone 01904 642315, www.york.ac.uk/inst/bihr). Published indexes, 1389-1688, are available at the Family Records Centre and the British National Archives. From 1653-60 this court was the only functioning probate body.

Surnames

The Guild of One-Name Studies, Box G, Society of Genealogists, 14 Charterhouse Buildings, Goswell Road, London EC1M 7BA (guild@one-name.org), regularly publishes its Register of One Name Studies. This is also available online at *http://www.one-name.org*.

Burial Records

In 2004 the Federation of Family History Societies published a National Burial Index (NBI) on CD-ROM, containing more than 13.2 million names of people buried over 4,300 churchyards and cemeteries in England and Wales between 1538 and 2000. Each entry includes the forename(s) and surname, date of burial, age (where given), the parish or cemetery where the event was recorded, and the family history group or society that transcribed the record. It does not include tombstone transcriptions. At present, coverage does not extend to every county, and the start and end dates vary from place to place, though it is particularly good for the period between 1813 and 1837. You can find out which places and periods are covered by visiting http://www.ffhs.org.uk/projects/overview.php

Parish Registers
Since 1538 clergy of the Anglican Church in England and in Wales have kept registers of church baptisms, marriages and burials. The local record office will be able to advise on their present whereabouts. The addresses of offices are included in Record Repositories in Great Britain (11th ed, 1999), and in **Record Offices: How to Find Them**, by J Gibson and P Peskett (Federation of Family History Societies, 9th ed 2002). You can also find details at: http://discovery.nationalarchives.gov.uk/details/a?_ref=105.

The Phillimore Atlas and Index of Parish Registers, edited by C Humphery-Smith (2nd ed, Chichester, 1995), lists parishes before 1832 county by county, the whereabouts of the registers, and if there are copies.

Wales
National Library of Wales, Aberystwyth, Wales SY23 3BU (Telephone 01970 632 800, email, holi@llgc.org.uk, web site, http://www.llgc.org.uk). This is the main centre for family history research in Wales, where you can inspect filmed copies of Welsh census returns, parish registers, nonconformist registers and probate records.

Scotland
General Register Office for Scotland, New Register House, 3 West Register Street, Edinburgh EH1 3YT (Telephone 0131 334 0380, email, records@gro-scotland.gov.uk web site, http://www.gro-scotland.gov.uk). The Registrar General holds records of civil registration of births, deaths and marriages from 1 January 1855 onwards, divorces, adoptions, decennial Scottish census returns, 1841-1901, and birth, baptism, marriage and burial registers of the Church of Scotland from about 1553 to 1854. the Family Records Centre has a computerized link to the GRO (Scotland) indexes to births, deaths and marriages, the birth, baptism and marriage registers, and to the 1881-1901 census returns. Full information can then be obtained by sending a completed application form and fee to the above address. Scottish Link is available by appointment, on payment of a fee (Telephone 020 7533 6438).

Alternatively, you can search online indexes to registered births up to 1901, deaths to 1951, and marriages to 1926, at http://www.scotlandspeople.gov.uk/ and then pay to view images of the birth (excluding 1855) and death records; images of the marriage entries are forthcoming. You can also search the indexes to the Church of Scotland (Old Parish Registers) births, baptisms and marriages between 1553 and 1854; indexes to the deaths and burials, and images of the registers are in the pipeline. Indexes and pay to view images are available for the 1891 and 1901 Scottish census returns at the same web site;

those of the decadal census returns from 1841 to 1881 will also be searchable soon. You can order transcriptions of the births, baptisms and marriages in the Old Parish Registers between 1700 and 1854, the registered births, marriages and deaths between 1855 and 1990, and of the 1861 and 1871 census returns by visiting *http://www.findmypast.co.uk/*.

Filmed copies of the birth, marriage and death civil registration indexes between 1855 and 1956, and parish registers between 1553 and 1854 can be found in the General Register Office for Scotland, *http://www.gro-scotland.gov.uk/*

The above Old Scottish Church Records are also available as part of FamilySearch, *http://www.familysearch.org/*. Try also the International Genealogical Index, and British Isles Vital Records Index.

National Archives of Scotland, HM General Register House, Princes Street, Edinburgh EH1 3YY (Telephone 0131 535 1314, email, enquiries@nas.gov.uk, web site, *http://www.nas.gov.uk*). A wide range of public records is held here, including wills and testaments from the 16th century to the present day. You can search indexes to Scottish wills and testaments between 1500 and 1875 at *http://www.scottishdocuments.com* and then purchase a copy of the digital images, which are in the process of being made available at the web site. Filmed copies of the indexes and testaments can be searched at Family History Centres, where a small fee may be payable to request a copy.

Ireland

General Register Office (Northern Ireland), Oxford House, 49-55 Chichester Street, Belfast BT1 4HL (Telephone 02890 252000, web site *https://www.welfare.ie/en/Pages/General-Register-Office.aspx*).

The Registrar General holds copies of the statutory registers of births and deaths since 1 January 1864, and marriages on and after 1 January 1922. You can search indexes to these, to non-Catholic marriages from 1 April 1845 and to all marriages from 1 January 1864 at this address, though the marriage registers to 1921 are kept in District Registrars' offices. A computerized index to births registered in Northern Ireland since 1922 is available at the Family Records Centre. Extracts of birth registrations from 1845 until 1875, and non-Catholic marriages between 1 April 1845 and 1863 are included in the International Genealogical Index . Filmed copies of the indexes and registers from 1922 to 1959 can be searched at Family History Centres. A small fee may be charged request a copy. For earlier filmed copies of indexes and registers see under the General Register Office, Dublin, below.

Public Record Office of Northern Ireland (PRONI) , 66 Balmoral Avenue, Belfast BT9 6NY (Telephone 02890 255905, email proni@dcalni.gov.uk, web site *http://www.proni.gov.uk/*). Most of the Irish census returns before 1901 were destroyed. You can search the 1901 census records of the Northern Irish counties, surviving fragments of the ten-yearly returns between 1821 and 1851, census substitutes, church and other denominational registers of births, baptisms, marriages and burials, and wills proved in Northern Ireland from

1900 to 1994. There are annual indexes to wills covering 1858 to 1984. Although all original wills prior to 1900 were destroyed, filmed office copies entered in local registry will books are available. Indexes to Irish wills, 1484-1858, can be searched on CD-ROM at the British National Archives and elsewhere.

General Register Office, Convent Road, Roscommon (Telephone +353(0)90 6632900), web site, *http://www.groireland.ie*). The Registrar General holds surviving indexed records of non-Roman Catholic marriages for the whole of Ireland from 1 April 1845 and of births, all marriages and deaths from 1 January 1864 up to 1921, and thereafter for Southern Ireland only. Copies of the indexes to 1958, birth registers for all Ireland up to the March quarter of 1881, 1900-13, and 1930-March quarter 1955, marriage registers from 1845 to 1870, and death registers 1864-70, can be inspected at Family History Centres.

National Archives of Ireland, Bishop Street, Dublin 8, Ireland (Telephone + 353 (0)1 407 2300, email, mail@nationalarchives.ie, web site, *http://www.nationalarchives.ie*). Holdings include the Irish census returns of 1901 and 1911, some transcripts for earlier years whose returns were destroyed in 1922, some Church of Ireland parish registers of baptisms, marriages and burials to 1871, indexes to wills proved in church courts up to 1858, original wills lodged in the Principal Registry in Dublin since 1904 and in most District Registries after 1900, and registered copies of most wills proved in District Registries since 1858. Microfilm copies of the 1901 and 1911 census returns can be searched at Family History Centres. Microfilm copies of most Roman Catholic registers up to at least 1880 can be searched at the National Library of Ireland, Kildare Street, Dublin 2, Ireland (Telephone +353 1 603 02 00, web site http://www.nli.ie). The Irish Family History Foundation is the co-coordinating body of a network of genealogical research centres, one serving every county. Visit *http://www.irishroots.net* for details.

Additional Resources:

In Search of Your British & Irish Roots, by Angus Baxter, Baltimore: Genealogical Publishing Co., 2000. *http://www.genealogical.com/*

The International Vital Records Handbook, by Thomas Jay Kemp, Baltimore: Genealogical Publishing Co., 2002. *http://www.genealogical.com/*

Ancestral Trails, The Complete Guide to British Genealogy and Family History, by Mark D. Herber, Baltimore: Genealogical Publishing Co., 1998. *http://www.genealogical.com/*

Tracing Your Irish Ancestors, 2nd Ed., by John Grenhem, Baltimore: Genealogical Publishing Co., 2002. *http://www.genealogical.com/*

Pocket Guide to Irish Genealogy, 2nd Ed., by Brian Mitchell, Baltimore: Genealogical Publishing Co., 2002. *http://www.genealogical.com/*

Germany

German immigrants began arriving on American shores as early as 1608 in Jamestown, Virginia. By the 18th Century, years of war, religious persecution and depravation drove thousands to cross the ocean. Many settled in Pennsylvania, Maryland, New York and the Carolinas. Germans became the largest national group to populate the United States.

Surnames

Bahlow, Ha ns. **Deutsches Namenlexikon.** Munich: Keysersche Verlagsbuchhandlung, 1967. (Ref 943 D4ba)

Brechenmacher, Josef Karlmann. **Deutsche Sippennamen.** Gorlitz: Verlag fur Sippenforschung und Wappenkunde C.A. Starke, 1936. (Ref 943 d4br pt. 1-2) (Film no. 492,908)

Brechenmacher, Josef Karlmann. **Etymologisches Worterbuch der Deutschen Familiennamen.** Limburg A.D. Lahn: C. A. Starke = Verlag, 1957. (Ref. 943 D4bj)

Parish Records

After you have determined the name of the kingdom, province, or duchy to which your ancestor's town belongs, you can locate the parish or civil registry that may contain birth, marriage and death records. This may be done by checking the following German gazetteer:

http://www.library.wisc.edu/etext/ravenstein/

Archive Guides

The following guides will help you find various regional archives and their holdings:

Verzeichnisse der Archivare. Neustadt/Aisch, Germany, Verlagsdruckerei, Ph. C. W. Schmidt, 1975.

Minerva-Handbucher, **Archive: Archive im deutschsprachigen Raum A - N Berlin**: Walter de Gruyter, 1974.

Additional Resources:

In Search of Your German Roots, by Angus Baxter, Baltimore: Genealogical Publishing Co., 2003. *http://www.genealogical.com/*

Encyclopedia of German-American Genealogical Research, by Clifford Neal Smith and Anna Piszczan-Czaja Smith, Baltimore: Genealogical Publishing Co., 2003. *http://www.genealogical.com/*

German-English Genealogical Dictionary, by Ernest Thode, Baltimore: Genealogical Publishing Co., 2003. *http://www.genealogical.com/*

The German Research Companion, by Shirley J. Riemer, Salt Lake City: Ancestry Publishing Co., 2000. *http://www.amazon.com/*

Italy

Italians did not impact U.S. immigration statistics until the late 19th century. In 1850, less than 4,000 Italians were reportedly in the U.S. However, in 1880, the population skyrocketed to 44,000, and by 1900, there were over 484,027. The majority of Italian immigrants arrived after 1876. Between 1884 and 1920 approximately 7 million Italians arrived on U.S. shores. Most Italian immigrants departed from Southern Italy and landed in New York City. Over the next 100 years, Italians made up the largest group of immigrants coming to America. Because many arrived after 1900, more complete records exist to aid Italian researchers. Prominent among these are the Ellis Island records.

Ellis Island

The Port of New York has for centuries been the most used portal to the United States for immigrants from around the world. While there were many other important entries into the country, it is estimated that more than 100 million Americans are directly related to immigrants who passed through Ellis Island during its tenure as a federal immigration station. Passenger manifest records were kept of the more than 22 million people who entered the United States through Ellis Island.

From 1892 to 1924, more than 22 million immigrants, passengers, and crew members came through Ellis Island and the Port of New York. The ship companies that transported these passengers kept detailed passenger lists, called ship manifests. Volunteers have transcribed these records and created a searchable database. If your ancestor was processed through Ellis Island during this time period, you may be able to find their record.

As with all transcribed databases, you must consider the many ways your ancestor's name could be spelled and misspelled on the passenger manifest or when transcribed. You may have to try many spelling variations before finding your ancestor. Information available on a passenger includes, name, ethnicity, date of arrival, age, gender, marital status, ship name and port of departure. This information can lead you to home town of your ancestor and vital records contained there.

The database can be searched for free at: *http://www.EllisIsland.org*

Italian Records

Modern Italian records were brought about during the Napoleonic era. Record keeping became more standardized throughout Italy. You will still find differences in the earlier years. Some may be kept on printed forms and others handwritten. When researching Southern Italy, you may find very clear and informative printed records as early as 1809. In the North they will still be hand written until about 1815. In the Trento area of Italy, after Napoleon left, civil records were kept by each local church parish, in addition to its own parish records. This procedure was continued until the area became part of the Italian Republic.

There are also variations in record-keeping found in the Piedmont area. Thus, the north presents problems for researchers, as opposed to the south and Sicily, where the vital records are much more uniform. Fortunately, the vast majority of immigrants to the United States came from the south and Sicily. Records are kept in the town hall by the town's ufficiale dello stato civile. It is his responsibility to make sure all events are recorded as required by law. A second copy is sent to Archivio di Stato. These records are not allowed by law to be seen by the public until they are over 75 years. A person or family member may view their own or that of their relative.

When requesting such records after 1860, asking for an extract rather than a certificate will potentially provide much more information. You may find parents' names, witnesses, etc. depending on the records requested.

Records needed before these time frames usually mean a search of church records. These records are not as informative or as accurate as those described above. These are kept in the local parish where they were originally written. In order for you to find these records you must know the comune and the church. This is easy when the comune is small and has one church. It becomes difficult when there is more than one church for the area, or several small comunes use one central church which may or may not be in the same town.

Parochial Records

Parochial archives contain information which in some cases might facilitate advancing a lineage into the 1400s. The earliest civil (vital statistics) records in Italy date only from the early 1800s, and census records provide only secondary information. Although pastors will sometimes allow direct access to the parochial archives in their care, they are not obligated to do so. A pastor may require his bishop's authorization before permitting a genealogist archival consultation. Even then, he might not permit the researcher to consult registers directly.

There are more dioceses in Italy than there are provinces, and bishops exercise ultimate authority over the parishes in their diocesan jurisdictions. Obtaining parochial archival access is quite time-consuming and often complicated, and may be influenced by a pastor's negative experience with discourteous amateur researchers. In some cases, a year or two can pass before a diocesan bishop decides to grant archival access for research purposes. This can impose a considerable and frustrating delay in completion of certain projects. Often, especially for periods before 1800, the information available in parochial records simply does not exist elsewhere.

The Family History Library in Salt Lake City has some Italian records. View their card catalog at: *http://www.familysearch.org*. Additionally, some baptism, birth, marriage and death records can be found on the International Genealogical Index (IGI) on the same site.

Civil Vital Records

Under Italian law, records of birth, marriages, and deaths are maintained by the Registrar of Vital Statistics (Ufficio della Stato civile) in the City Office (Comune or Municipio) of the place where the event occurred. There is no central, regional or provincial office which keeps such records. When Napoleon took over most of Italy in the beginning of the nineteenth century, the French instituted a system of law, which included the recording of civil vital statistics. This system introduced new forms for the recording of births, marriages, and deaths (these forms are similar to the forms used for the registration of these events today).

Italian registrars are not required by law to assist in genealogical research work. In most places, records dating back as far as the mid-19th century are available but unless complete and correct information is provided, no search can be undertaken. If you are engaged in family tree reconstruction and do not have the essential information bearing on your ancestors, you may wish to retain the aid of professional researchers. A separate list of firms or individuals specializing in genealogical work (ancestry, coat of arms, etc) is available on the Association of Professional Genealogists website at: *https://www.apgen.org/*

To determine what records exist for a specific Comune, visit: *http://www.sersale.org/comunes.htm*

Additional Resources:

Finding Italian Roots, 2nd Ed., by John Philip Colleta, Baltimore: Genealogical Publishing Co., 2003. *http://www.genealogical.com/*

Italian Genealogical Records: How to Use Italian Civil, Ecclesiastical, & Other Records in Family History Research, by Trafford R. Cole, Salt Lake City: Ancestry Publishing, 1995. *http://www.amazon.com/*

Italian-American Family History, by Sharon DeBartolo Carmack, Baltimore: Genealogical Publishing Co., 1997. *http://www.genealogical.com/*

Italian Surnames, by Joseph G. Fucilla, Baltimore: Genealogical Publishing Co., 2003. *http://www.genealogical.com/*

Chapter Action Plan
- Determine as much information as possible about your immigrant ancestor using U.S. resources before attempting overseas research
- Use passenger lists and other immigration resources to determine from what country and what province or county your ancestor immigrated
- Try to find your ancestor's home town, village, or parish to narrow your records search to a small area
- Using the Internet, determine what records are available for your ancestor and where they are archived
- Try to search on-line databases and obtain copies by emailing or writing the appropriate archive
- If you don't speak the language or cannot travel to a foreign country, consider hiring a local professional researcher to dig for hard-to-find information and records

Chapter 19
Hiring Professional Genealogists

Trees without roots fall over
--Anonymous

There always comes a time in every family history researcher's life when you hit the proverbial "brick wall". No matter what you try, nothing seems to work in getting you past the wall and on to adding one more generation to your family line. As you can imagine, you may someday reach a point where you cannot go back in time any further with a particular line, but that probably won't happen for a long time.

If you reach a sticky point, it may be time to bring in a professional who can review your work with fresh eyes and make recommendations or provide additional research to help you find the answer.

We will review what professionals can offer, where to find them and what to expect.

Define Your Goals

As with your own research, you must determine what you want a professional to do for you. A few objectives may include the following:
- Research a specific courthouse or archive for a specific piece of information, such as a will, marriage record or baptism.
- Assist you in becoming a member of a lineage society, such as the DAR or SAR.
- Work with foreign records that you cannot read or translate.
- Search cemeteries where your ancestor may be buried.
- Assist you with locating living relatives, such as birth parents, siblings or distant relatives to establish a family association.

As you can tell from the above objectives, the time and money involved can vary significantly. If you have only a limited budget for professional research, you must narrow your search and focus on one target at a time.

Professional Specialties

As you search for a professional to assist you, determine if you need a specialist to meet your objectives. Most professionals are generalists and cover common U.S. or International research problems. However, others may specialize in areas that may help in your particular situation. A few specialties may include:
- Heraldry
- Ethnic groups
- Overseas research
- Research in specific time periods
- Lineage society applications

Document specialists who work with state, regional or national archives can be especially helpful when you are trying to located records that have been damaged by fire, flood, war or neglect. They may be able to find alternative copies or other records that can be substituted. You can also hire professionals who work in the Family History Library in Salt Lake City. They have access to records from all over the world and may save you time and money in finding your immigrant family without ever having to leave the U.S. or deal with foreign governments.

Finding a Pro

Fortunately, there are associations that accredit and monitor professional genealogists, both in the U.S. and abroad. Even though you are never guaranteed that your professional will follow ethical standards, the associations can help limit your search to accredited genealogists who have agreed to follow a code of ethics. If things go badly, you have a place to take your complaints if you feel you have not been treated fairly. The three top groups promoting professional practices include:

The Association of Professional Genealogists (APG),
http://www.apgen.org
The Board for Certification of Genealogists (BCG),
http://www.bcgcertification.org
The International Commission for the Accreditation of Professional Genealogists (ICAPGen*), http://www.icapgen.org*

All groups require members to follow a code of ethics and standards of professionalism. They can provide you a list of certified or accredited members, their area of specialty and contact information.

Certifications

Most professionals have become certified in the course of their professional careers. They strive to increase their skills and knowledge to better serve their potential clients. Some of the most popular certifications include the following:

Certified Genealogical Records Specialist (CGRS). The CGRS excels in searches of original and derivative records; is an expert in genealogical sources relating to, but not limited to, his or her chosen areas of specialization; and provides detailed information on the contents of records examined. BCG certification

Certified Lineage Specialist (CLS). The CLS conducts research to reconstitute a single line of direct parent-to-child descent from an individual in the past and is adept in appraising the authenticity of both original and derivative sources as they apply to the line of descent. The CLS may specialize in hereditary-society applications or in determining descent from a historical Indian tribe indigenous to North America. BCG certification

Certified Genealogist (CG). The CG is proficient in all areas of genealogical research and analysis, is qualified to solve relationship and identity

problems of all types, and is experienced in the compilation of well-crafted family histories. BCG certification.
Accredited Genealogist (AG). The AG must take proctored examinations after demonstrating sufficient practical background and experience. Separate tests and testing methods (written reports, essay questions, foreign language abilities, oral exams, and case study solutions) are given for each geographical area and subject of specialization. ICAPGen certification.

Hiring a Pro
Once you have determined your research objective and budget, it is time to contact a few professionals who have the specialty, location or certification you feel will best meet your goals. Follow these steps:
- Briefly state your research issue, including research you have already completed. State specifically what you want the professional to find.
- Agree on an hourly fee in writing and an estimate on how much time will be needed to complete the assigned task. Determine if you must provide a retainer or be billed after the research is completed.
- Provide the researcher with your family group sheets, pedigree charts, research notes and copies of documents related to the assigned task. Include all pieces of information that may aid the researcher and prevent duplication of your efforts.

Once the professional has reviewed your materials, they may have additional questions or ask you in what format you would like the results, such as paper, electronic, GEDCOM, etc. If you want both copies of original documents and abstracts or translations the cost may be more.

Agree on a timetable for updates and for further research. Are you willing to continue paying the researcher after the initial amount is exhausted, or do you want a final report before spending more money?

Regardless of the results, insist on a final report and copies of all documents researched. Even if your research problem is not solved, you will know what has been done and avoid going back over the same records later.

Understand that there are no guarantees. The researcher may or may not solve your problem, but must be paid according to your agreement.

Chapter Action Plan
- Exhaust all research avenues yourself, before turning to a professional genealogist
- Determine specifically what task you want the professional to complete for you
- Use professional associations, local genealogical societies and fellow researchers to find a good professional in the locale and specialty you need
- Obtain a written agreement as to costs, time, reporting, and other criteria before contracting with the professional and paying fees

Chapter 20
Genealogy and DNA

I think that I shall never see a completed genealogy.
--Unknown

DNA testing has been around for some time now and used extensively in criminal investigations to tie a potential suspect to a crime. However, recent improvements in home DNA tests and a reduction in lab costs have generated a new interest in family history studies and linking past generations to the present.

DNA Fingerprints
Human DNA carries the genetic codes to re-create ourselves through reproduction. Each parent provides 23 chromosomes which pair up to determine the genetic makeup of the child. The last pair is designated by the letters X or XY. Females have two X chromosomes and males have one X and one Y. During fertilization, each parent's chromosomes are combined and redistributed, except the Y chromosome. A male's Y chromosome comes entirely from his father. As a result, except for rare genetic mutations, every male carries the same Y-DNA pattern as his father, his paternal grandfather, and all other male ancestors in the direct line back to the beginning of human evolution.

Y-DNA testing was used recently in the famous Jefferson-Hemings study, which found that at least one of the lines descended from President Thomas Jefferson's slave Sally Hemings, was also descended from a male Jefferson. Other research determined that President Jefferson was the most likely father.

Another study of a 9000 year old skeleton in Cheddar, England found a male descendent still living in the region today. This same technique will be used to determine if Neanderthals, who died out over 25,000 years ago, can be linked to modern humans.

Mitochondrial DNA (mtDNA)
Mitochondrial are tiny globules that are found in each human cell, outside the central nucleus where chromosomal DNA is found. This DNA is not affected by the dividing and combining of chromosomes that takes place at fertilization and is passed on unchanged to all offspring, both male and female. However, a male cannot pass on his mtDNA to his offspring, only the female can do this. As a result, your mtDNA is the same as your mother's, which is the same as her mother's and so on. If two people have the same mtDNA, then they probably shared a common maternal ancestor; but it cannot be determined if this ancestor lived recently or hundreds of years ago.

Application to Genealogy

How can DNA testing assist in finding ancestors on your family tree? Some of the possibilities include:
- Determining the genetic relationship of two people
- Linking a common ancestor to living individuals
- Determining if individuals with the same surname are related
- Mapping the origins of large population groups

If you are researching a common ancestor with another individual, you can determine if the two of you are related by a common male ancestor (Y-DNA) or of you have a common female ancestor (mtDNA). If a match is found, additional individuals will need to be tested to narrow down which ancestor is common. If you submit your results to a commercial DNA database, you may find related individuals anywhere in the world that share a common ancestor. This may help you find the country, even town of origin for your immigrant ancestor. This can be especially helpful if little or no records exist to prove ancestry to the home country, such as is common in research undertaken by slave descendents.

DNA Databases

As DNA testing has become more reliable, firms have been established to create large databases that will help individuals connect with ancestors and with other living descendants.

Today there are over 7 billion people living on the planet. If we go back just 30 generations (~750 years), we should each have over 1 billion ancestors. However, scientists estimate there were only 400 million people alive on earth in 1250 AD. Additionally, not all of those individuals had descendants that survived to produce their own children. As a result, we all share common ancestors and all people in the world are related to each other in varying degrees. The goal of commercial databases is to establish links to those common ancestors and tie them to their living descendants.

AncestryDNA

AncestryDNA is the leader in DNA testing for family history and includes more than 3 million people who have taken the AncestryDNA test as well as the ability to access Ancestry, the world's largest online family history resource, which includes millions of family trees and over 19 billion historical records.

AncestryDNA results include information about your ethnicity across 26 regions/ethnicities and identifies potential relatives through DNA matching to others who have taken the AncestryDNA test. Your results are a great starting point for more family history research, and it can also be a way to dig even deeper into the research you've already done.

https://www.ancestry.com/dna/

Y-Search

Started in 2000, this database contains the test results of over 5,000 records. The firm accepts test results from any testing service and adds the results to the database for public research. *http://www.ysearch.org/*

23andMe

23andMe, much like AncestryDNA, analyzes your DNA and provides you with an array of information about your ancestry. To date, 23andMe has collected DNA from more than a million people. The two services use similar DNA collection kits for about the same price, but 23andMe gives you more details about your ancestry, diving into your maternal and paternal lines, and even back to the Neanderthals.

https://www.23andme.com/

DNA Surname Study

If you decide to manage a surname study to determine links to a common ancestor or clan, here are some guidelines to follow:

Define your goals and objectives. Do you wish to prove connection to a common ancestor or determine the relationship of many individuals with the same surname?

Select a testing center. You should pick a center that offers the services you need to track, record and analyze your testing results. Some centers only test, while others provide a database and comparative analysis. If you plan on including many individuals in your test, you may be able to negotiate a lower price per test.

Find you test subjects. How are you going to locate and test the individuals in your group? Will it be restricted to a small number of fellow researchers or do you want to include a wider pool? You may need to work with a surname mailing list or create a web site to recruit members for your test.

Manage the project. Keep your subjects updated with lab results and other data. A website may be a useful communication tool. If you have selected a testing center that provides analysis, you might consider a direct link to their site from yours. Honor privacy concerns before you make test results public or publish results.

Additional firms providing DNA tests:

African Ancestry, *http://www.africanancestry.com/*
Ancestry by DNA, *https://www.ancestrybydna.com/*
Family Tree DNA, *http://www.familytreedna.com/*
MyHeritageDNA, *https://www.myheritage.com/dna*

Chapter Action Plan
- If you plan on using DNA testing in your research, map out your goals, methods and management process
- Determine if you need to include a small group in your testing pool or a large one. Similar large-scale projects may already be underway
- Contact a lab that can provide the services you need and instruct your test subjects to send in samples for testing
- Manage your project by providing periodic reports, test results and conclusions based on test results

Chapter 21
Publishing Your Work

We learn from history that we do not learn from history
--Anonymous

The goal of most family researchers is to someday publish their research and share their hard work with the rest of the world. After years of research, you will want to preserve your findings for future generations. Once you have gathered enough material for a book, there are many questions you must answer before delivering your baby to the world.

Today, publishing can take many forms, including the traditional printed book. In order to determine the best way to reach your audience, you must think about who they are.

Target Audience

Most books are a collaboration of many researchers working together to complete sections of the family tree. As an example, you and other researchers are each assigned a child of your great-grandfather. The work will involve tracing the descendants of each of his children to the present and connecting them to living relatives.

Other projects may involve compiling information on a community's pioneers and some of their descendants. Here the target audience would include anyone whose ancestor may have lived in the community. Many books are limited to a small family association and a common ancestor. In this example, your book may appeal only to those members. The determination of your target audience will help you select the format to publish your work.

Formats

Today's technology provides us a multitude of ways to produce compiled family history research. Just a few include:
- Traditional offset press
- E-book
- CD-ROM/DVD
- Family Website
- GEDCOM

We will look at the pros and cons of each option and what it may mean to you.

Traditional Offset Press

Almost all printed books today are produced by offset press. This method creates a master plate which is used to print the actual pages. By far, the most common and the most long-lasting, this method allows you to produce books that can be distributed to hundreds or thousands of people, plus libraries and archives all over the world. Your research would be preserved for generations to come. It is critical that acid-free paper be used to print your book to preserve it for future researchers. However, printed books are also expensive, normally requiring a minimum press run, binding and shipping costs. If you want to add photos, graphics or copies of documents, the cost is higher. However, if your target group is not computer savvy, this may be the only choice.

Many companies cater to the family history publisher, providing help at all stages of the process. Before you get to far in your publishing adventure, contact several and ask for sample prices, procedures and tips on making the printing process as easy as possible. Before you have 500 copies made of your masterpiece, you might want to circulate pre-order forms with projected book prices and get an indication of interest. You may find that only 200 books will be needed. Some of the options you will need to consider for your book include:

- Hard or soft cover
- Book Size (8.5 x 11, 5.5 x 8.5, etc)
- Cover design
- Four-color or two-color cover printing
- Photographs and other graphics
- Paper stock
- Initial run size
- Fulfillment

These decisions will directly impact the final cost of your book. If you must order a large quantity and they do not sell, you could be stuck with an expensive paperweight. Work with you printer to minimize surprises and produce the right quantity for your needs.

Here is a list of short run publishers that specialize in genealogy related books. They can provide a wealth of information about the choices you have in bringing your book to completion:

Outskirts Press, *https://outskirtspress.com/*
Accent Group Solutions,
http://accentgroupsolutions.com/
The Gregath Publishing Company, *http://www.gregathcompany.com/index.html*

E-Books

If you find that many of your potential customers have access to a computer and the Internet, you may be able to deliver a book to them at a reduced price. Electronic books, or E-Books are quickly catching on with authors who want to provide up-to-the-minute material delivered by email or file downloads. It is estimated that over 1,000,000 E-Books are produced each year, many by self-publishers who are catering to a niche market.

Using a common word processing program such as Microsoft Word, you prepare your manuscript, including color photographs, documents and other material that would be cost prohibitive with traditional printing. The file is then converted to a common file format, such as epub which can be opened by hundreds of users with different computer operating systems and software. There are special portable e-book readers that allow your customer to take his or her book to the park or any comfortable location.

You can either handle payment, fulfillment and technical support, or allow e-book publishers to provide these services for a fee or a percent of each sale. You can email your family members the website and they can order online and receive their book instantly. You have the option of permitting buyers to print your book once it resides on their computer. If you plan both an e-book and a traditional book, you might not want to allow this feature. You can even sell your e-book on Amazon.com. They will pay you a small royalty for every book sold!

E-book publishing is still in its infancy and many companies have come and gone. A short list of a few current publishers is listed below. They can provide assistance in getting your e-book to the market:

Booklocker.com, *http://www.booklocker.com/*
Lulu.com, *http://www.lulu.com/*
Book Baby, *https://www.bookbaby.com/*
Amazon Kindle Direct Publishing, *https://kdp.amazon.com*

Family Website

Family websites are becoming more popular with the increased use of personal home computers. The costs of web page hosting and storage have dropped over the years and many more individuals now have access to the Internet. You may create your family website for many reasons, including the following:

- Central site for multiple researchers working on a common ancestor
- Compare notes with other researchers
- Provide family access to current research, photographs and other data
- Publish a family association newsletter or make other announcements
- Provide a way for other family members to update latest births, marriages, deaths, etc. that have occurred in the family
- Upload GEDCOMs and other family data for viewing by other members

Regardless of your reasons for starting a site, you will want to consider the level of technical skills needed for such an undertaking. If you are not sufficiently skilled in website design, you may want to find someone in the family with needed skills, or hire a firm to build your site. There are many web hosts who will provide basic templates and instruction for you to build your own. Today, many firms can offer complete website hosting services or just the services you need to complete your project. You can require password entry into your site if you want to restrict the information to immediate family. You would email the password only to those you want to access the site.

The following firms offer website design and hosting for family history researchers:

Family WebHost, *http://www.familywebhost.com/*
Ancestors-Genealogy.com, *http://www.ancestors-genealogy.com/*
Tribal Pages.com, *http://www.tribalpages.com/*

GEDCOM

As discussed in Chapter 14, GEDCOMS are the universal translators of the genealogy world. These files allow you to share your information with others in the hopes of building a larger family tree. If you are not quite ready to complete a book on your family, or want to "test the waters" and see if your data can generate interest from other researchers, you might want to start by publishing a GEDCOM of some of your work.

Most genealogy database software programs allow you to create GED-COMS of some or all of your family lines with as many or few generations as you desire. Once you have selected your included database, the GEDCOM is created and saved to your hard drive with a descriptive file name, such as Smith01.ged or Jones2004.ged so you can differentiate it from other similar files. If your software program does not automatically include source material, you must insure that this is included. GEDCOMS without source material are not to be trusted. It would be like a scientist publishing his new hypothesis without including any test results or mathematical equations to prove his theory. He might as well be writing a science fiction novel...no one will trust the results!

Many databases have been created to store, maintain and provide access to submitted GEDCOM files. These databases can be a source of new material for your research and a portal for you to submit your findings to the world to review:

RootsWeb.com, *http://www.rootsweb.com/*
Genealogy.com, *http://www.genealogy.com/*
Mytrees.com, *http://www.mytrees.com/*
FamilySearch.org, *http://www.familysearch.org/*
OneGreatFamily.com, *http://www.onegreatfamily.com/*
Ancestry.com, *http://www.ancestry.com/*

What do you include in your book?

Sometimes the hardest decision is what to include in your book and what to leave out. It is very easy to get carried away with stories about great-grandpa Mike and his childhood in Nebraska. However, keep in mind your book must appeal not only to immediate family, but others who have never heard of great-grandpa Mike. They are interested if your research can help them with a problem in their family history. The trick is creating a balance between family tradition and genealogical research.

One of the best ways to help achieve this balance is reading other family history books that have received awards or honors as quality publications. Many genealogical publications provide reviews of newly published family history books. Read several of these reviews in past issues at your local library or historical society. Pick out 4 or 5 books that interest you and find them on the book shelf. If they are not available locally, you may be able to borrow them through interlibrary loan. Read each book, looking at contents, organization, material, sources, photographs and other details. Consider all the elements you would value when reviewing a book and use these guidelines in your own publication. Always remember your target audience and future generations who will read your masterpiece!

Conclusion
As you begin your journey, remember that you will never have a complete genealogy. Your work will be the foundation that later generations will build on. You are leaving a valuable legacy for future researchers to appreciate. As with any hobby, moderation is the key. If you spend all your time at the library or on the computer, you will lose spending precious time with your loved ones. Good luck and happy hunting!

Chapter Action Plan
- Before writing you book, determine your target audience
- Determine what format and how many copies you need to determine initial costs
- Research many publishers and printing firms to discover methods of submitting your manuscript and what services they can offer you
- Once your book is published, provide copies to libraries, historical societies and other repositories where others may be researching the same family lines
- Keep updating your material and publish revised editions as needed
- Have fun!

Glossary

Abstract – a summary of relevant facts and names of a document or report
Affidavit – a document written under oath in the presence of court officials or other authorized persons representing a statement of facts
Administrator – person appointed by the court to manage the division of assets for a deceased's estate who died without a will
Alien – a foreigner or citizen of another country See also Immigrant
Ancestor – a person from whom you descend; a forefather
Archives – A repository of records, normally governmental or institutional
Banns – public statement of the intent to marry
Bequeath – to transfer ownership of personal property in a will
Biography – an account of a person's life written by someone other than the subject
Bond – a binding agreement to perform certain duties normally related to court procedures, such as estate settlement, etc. The individual would be required to pay a sum of money as a penalty for failure to complete the task
Bounty land – land awarded or promised for military service
Census – an official listing or counting of the population of the country, state or region See enumeration
Christian name – the name given at baptism or christening, given name
Circa – Latin for about or around. Used before a date when exact time is not known, circa 1800 or c1800
Codicil – a supplement or addition to a will
Collateral lines – people with whom you share no immediate genetic relationship, but who have married into common ancestral lines
Conveyances – transfer of property from one person to another
Consort – wife or husband whose spouse is living; spouse of a monarch
Consanguinity – two individuals who share a common ancestor; relationship by blood
Declaration of Intention – the first paper filed by an alien in court to become a citizen
Deed – title to a property; transfer of ownership of a property
Descendant – child, grandchild, etc. of an individual
Devise – to give property such as land in a will
Dower – legal right of a wife to a portion of her deceased husband's lands or tenements
Emigrant – a person who leaves his or her native country to live in another
Enumeration – a counting or listing, such as a census
Estate – the personal, real property and debts belonging to a person
Executor – an individual appointed in a will by the testator to carry out the provisions of the will
Extract – the verbatim transcription of a portion of a document or record
Fee Simple – private ownership in real estate in which the owner has the right to control, use and transfer the property at will
Gazetteer – a geographic dictionary or index listing place names and descriptions.

Glossary

GEDCOM – an acronym for GEnealogical Data COMmunication. A file format used to share genealogical data with other researchers who not use the same application
Grantee – one who buys property or receives a grant or conveyance
Grantor – one who sells a property or makes a grant or conveyance
Guardian – person appointed to care for and manage the property of a minor, orphan or incompetent adult
Gregorian calendar – In 1582 Pope Gregory XIII ordered a replacement to the Julian calendar. Most Protestant countries did not convert until 1752. Established standards used today such as leap years, etc. See Julian calendar
Heir – one entitled by law or by will to inherit property from another
Immigrant – an alien moving into a country from another with intent to live there
Indentured servant – one bound into the service of another person for a specified number of years in exchange for learning a trade or for travel expenses
Intestate – one who dies without a will
Issue – offspring; progeny; children
Julian calendar – named for Julius Caesar and used from 45 B.C. to A.D. 1582. Some countries did not convert to the Gregorian calendar until 1752. See Gregorian calendar
Legacy – property or money left to someone in a will
Lineage – your direct descent from a particular ancestor
Loyalist – An American colonist who supported the British side in the American Revolution; Tory
Maiden name – a woman's family name before marriage; birth name
Majority – legal age; adult status
Militia – Citizen army; not part of a national army
Nee – French for born; used to indicate a woman's maiden name
Patent – grant of land from a government to an individual
Pedigree – your family tree or lineage; ancestry
Pension – money paid to an individual, widow or orphan by a government for wartime military service
Pole – a measure of 16 1/2 feet in length used in land surveys; rod or perch
Poll – list of residents such as a voting list or tax list. Example: poll tax
Primary record – the original document created by an eyewitness at or near the time of the event. Examples include birth certificate, marriage certificate or death certificate
Primogeniture – the right of the eldest child to inherit the entire estate of the parents
Probate – the legal process of settling the estate of the deceased
Public domain – land owned or controlled by the government
Quitclaim deed – transfer of claim or title without guarantee of valid title
Relict – widow
Secondary record – a record created some time after an event or created from other sources

Glossary

Section – 640 acres or 1/36 division of a township in the rectangular survey system
Sibling – a person having one or both parents in common with another; brother or sister
Source – an item or document relating to a person or event; information used to prove a fact or theory
Source citation – A detailed list of information about a source listed on reports and charts
Surname – family name or last name
Testator – the person who makes a valid will before death
Vital records – civil records such as birth, marriage, divorce or death
Warranty deed – a deed in which the seller of the property guarantees a clear title to the buyer
Will – a document providing instructions for the division of property after death

Index

A
Accredited Genealogist (AG), 87
Analyzing Census Data, 35
AncestryDNA, 90

B
Birth Records, 25
Bounty Land Records, 45

C
Cemetery Types and Locations, 63
Certified Genealogical Records Specialist (CGRS), 86
Certified Genealogist (CG), 86
Certified Lineage Specialist (CLS), 86
Church Records Survey, 54
Church Records, 54
Computerized Resources, 21
Confederate Pension Records, 45

D
DAR Patriot Index, 71
Date and Place Name Formats, 16
Daughters of the American Revolution (DAR), 72
Death Records, 27
DNA Databases, 90
DNA Fingerprints, 89
DNA Surname Study, 91
Documentation, 8

E
E-Books, 94
Ellis Island, 81
England & British Isles, 76

F
Family Associations, 68
Family Website, 95
FamilySearch.org, 61
Federal and State Land Records, 47
Formats, 93
Forms and Formats, 15
Free On-Line Databases, 60

G
GEDCOM, 58
Genealogical Societies, 68
Genealogical Software, 57
Genealogy and DNA, 89
GENTECH, 70
Germany, 80
Glossary, 98
GPS Technology, 64

H
Hiring Professional Genealogists, 85

I
Immigrant Ancestors, 75
Immigration and Naturalization, 37
Index of Revolutionary War Pension Applications in the National Archives, 43
Interlibrary Loan, 20
Internet GEDCOM, 24
Ireland, 78
Italy, 81

Index

L

Land records, 28
Library Resources and Guidance, 19
Lineage Societies, 71

M

Marriage Records, 26
Microfilm and Microform Records, 20
Military, 41
Mitochondrial DNA (mtDNA), 89
Mortality Schedules, 35

N

National Archives Records, 31
National Society of the Sons of the American Revolution (SAR), 72
New York Genealogical and Biographical Society (NYG&B), 70
Numbering Systems, 14

O

On-line Passenger Lists, 38

P

Parochial Records, 82
Patent Process, 50
Pension Records, 43
Probate Records, 27
Professional Specialties, 85
Proper Census Research Methods, 34
Publishing Your Work, 93

R

Recording the Interview, 10
Research in the Land Entry Files of the General Land Office, Record Group 49, 52
RootsWeb.com, 61

S

Scotland, 77
Ship Passenger Arrival Records, 37
Software Programs, 58
Source Citations, 23
State Census Records, 35
State Land Patents, 48
Survey System of Federal Land States, 49

T

The National Genealogical Society (NGS), 70
The New England Historic Genealogical Society, 69
The USGenWeb Project, 62
Tract Books, 51
Traditional Offset Press, 93

W

Wales, 77
Wikipedia, 62
Write Your Autobiography, 7

Y

Y-Search, 91

CPSIA information can be obtained
at www.ICGtesting.com
Printed in the USA
LVOW10s1537280118
564334LV00011B/525/P